12

EASY STEPS

TO CHANGE

YOUR LIFE

12

EASY STEPS

TO **CHANGE**

YOUR **LIFE**

STOP WAITING FOR THAT *BIG THING!*

BRIAN PROCTOR

Published 2024 by Gildan Media LLC
aka G&D Media
www.GandDmedia.com

Front cover design by David Rheinhardt of Pyrographx

Interior design by Meghan Day Healey of Story Horse, LLC

Library of Congress Cataloging-in-Publication Data is available upon
request

ISBN: 978-1-7225-0694-0

10   9   8   7   6   5   4   3   2   1

To my loving wife, Cory Kelly Proctor,
my biggest cheerleader. Her efforts have made
this book far better than how it started out.
She has a gift with words and a work ethic
to be admired. I love my life with you.

CONTENTS

INTRODUCTION

Many people spend their lives waiting for that one big thing. They dream of the single moment that will change their life forever. They often look for fast solutions like buying lottery tickets or online "get rich quick" schemes, hoping for an instant transformation.

The abundance of information at our fingertips from various sources, including social media—coupled with the instant feedback we receive from our digital devices—has changed our expectations. We often believe our goals should be achieved overnight, leading to impatience and frustration.

It's time to STOP for a moment and challenge this thinking about overnight success. Are you ready to try something different? Are you seeking a better life for yourself and your family? Would you like to move on a strategy that's not some new gimmick, but actually works and has stood the test of time?

Here's the bigger question. Could you be willing to entertain the paradox that when you stop trying to force instant results from that big thing, only then will incredible results come naturally and more expediently?

What I am about to share with you in this book is simple, though it requires intentional, consistent effort—and a shift in mindset.

This mindset shift will include finding your inner peace. I'll bet that sounds good right about now, doesn't it? In my life, I've discovered that operating from a place of calm accelerates my successes because it allows me to stay fully aware and focused in the present moment—instead of wasting precious time and energy feeling overwhelmed with my attention dispersed in the many facets of the past and future.

You can achieve great things by simply taking care of the little things. If you dedicate time each day to doing something small that moves you closer to your goal, you'll find that, often sooner than expected, you will reach that big milestone.

In fact, focusing on one small task each day adds up to 365 accomplishments over a year. I promise you that amounts to something significant. The key is to concentrate on what is in front of you and let those efforts build day by day.

This approach is truly the best way to live. It is guaranteed to help you stay focused and prevent overwhelm. By bringing your attention to the present moment and understanding the impact of daily actions, no matter how small, you will achieve much more in a shorter period of time, leading to a better, calmer, and more peaceful life. Success on the wings of happiness and calmness is possible for all of us.

This is the central message I want to convey in this book. Let's make happy and calm your new normal. Say hello to a new you!

By exploring the principles and strategies outlined in these pages, you'll uncover new perspectives and actionable techniques for personal and professional development, which will lead to a better, happier, and more fulfilling life. Whether your burning desire is to boost your career, start a business, improve your relationships, or cultivate inner peace, this book offers simple yet extremely effective tools and wisdom to support you and again—they've been proven to work. Embrace them to transform your dreams into reality and embark on a simple path toward a more purposeful and joyful existence.

With dedication and the right approach, you can unlock your full potential and live a life that truly resonates with your deepest values and desires. The end result is a life well lived that includes a sense of freedom that you perhaps never dreamed possible for yourself. Won't it be great to reach the end and reflect on your journey with a feeling of, "Wow, I had no idea my life would be THIS great"—instead of looking back at a laundry list of regrets and what-ifs?

Change is inevitable—in fact, gigantic changes are happening all around us every day. But your own personal growth that will allow you to keep up with the new world, well, that's NOT inevitable. It's a choice. A choice you must make if you desire to be free and live the good life.

A Legacy of Personal Growth

My name is Brian Proctor, and I've lived a rare, fortunate life immersed in the world of personal development. This journey began for me on the day I was born in December of 1961. The principles laid out in this book are the blueprint of my life. They were gifted to me by my father, and now I'm delighted to gift them to you.

My father was Bob Proctor, a renowned speaker, author, coach, and thought leader. In 2006, at the age of seventy-two, his time in the spotlight finally came when his trainings rocketed onto the world stage with the movie phenomenon *The Secret*. What followed included multiple appearances on *Larry King Live*, *The Ellen DeGeneres Show*, *Nightline*, and more.

For decades leading up to his movie and TV debut, my father lived and taught the principles of success. He was a pioneer in this area decades before it became what we know it as today. It's important to note that my father was not born into wealth and prosperity. In fact, his life started out immersed in poverty and amid a world war.

After many struggles that continued into his late twenties, he met a man by happenstance who introduced him to a book that forever changed him. Dad went on to completely turn his life around in every way, and thereafter he became positively obsessed with spending the rest of his life—sixty years, in fact—helping people around the world from every possible background realize their unadulterated, unlimited potential.

Throughout those sixty years, quite literally starting with my very first breath, I absorbed his experiences and wisdom—and for nearly thirty of them, I had the privilege of working by his side. Growing up with Bob Proctor as my father, friend, and mentor gave me a unique understanding of life and provided me with invaluable insights about how health, wealth, and success of all kinds works.

After my father passed away in 2022, I felt a profound responsibility and honor to continue his work in my own voice. His life and teachings have left an indelible mark on countless lives worldwide, and my mission is to continue that incredible momentum by sharing the wisdom he imparted to me, not only through his intentional teachings, but through decades of direct observation. Bob Proctor was a man who practiced what he preached, even behind closed doors—and in my experience, that's rare.

Attitude Is the Magic Word

One of the earliest lessons I learned from my father was the power of attitude. As a young boy in the mid-1960s when technology was still relatively simple, I remember car rides with Dad where he would play Earl Nightingale's famous recording, "The Magic Word," which was immersed with teachings on one's attitude. Holding a portable record player with a rotating black disc in one hand while driving with the other, he would play that lecture over and over. This repetitive exposure to Nightingale's teachings, plus witnessing my father model them firsthand, ingrained in me the importance of maintaining a positive attitude—a lesson that has shaped my life profoundly.

The biggest takeaway on attitude that I want to share with you today is that we have the power to choose how we respond to life's ups and downs. We should accept and treat them casually, much like our attitude toward the ebb and flow of tides—or the rising and setting of the sun. Understanding this has allowed me to navigate life's lows with a good attitude, knowing that the tide will turn—after a down, or even a series of downs, up has to come around the corner. It's a natural law of the Universe. I hope knowing this provides great comfort to you.

Our circumstances, no matter how dreary, do not have to dictate our outlook. We can and should sustain a positive attitude regardless of what is happening around us. When we choose to see the world positively, the world responds in kind, and opportunities for growth and success become more apparent—by sheer fact that we're looking for them. In fact, when we master this, not only are we looking for these opportunities—even better, we're expecting them to come along and know they are available to us.

What would happen if you walked through your life every day with the attitude of, "something wonderful is about to happen"?

As Earl Nightingale said in that famous record, "We become what we think about most of the time." It's our responsibility and privilege to take ownership of our thoughts and make a conscious effort at shifting them to the positive as a form of habit.

Lessons from the Bricklayer

In my twenties during my commute to work in Toronto, I recall watching bricklayers do their job. They would meticulously lay one brick at a time, focusing on the task at hand. This process, though seemingly slow, would result in the completion of an entire house relatively quickly. The key was their commitment to the process, focus, and patience—all qualities that are essential for achieving long-term success. Another quality was that they had faith in the process and never doubted that their effort would yield a completed house.

Similarly, our goals may seem distant, but by breaking them down into manageable tasks and focusing on one step at a time, maintaining faith that we'll achieve them, we can make remarkable progress. This approach reduces the feeling of overwhelm and keeps you moving forward while making positive, productive headway.

I remember how the bricklayers never rushed. They placed each brick carefully to ensure the structure's stability and strength. This taught me that success isn't about speed; it's about consistency and precision.

Whether you're building a career or business, nurturing a relationship, or working on yourself, the same principles apply. By dedicating yourself to small, deliberate actions, and maintaining faith in the process, you lay a solid foundation for future achievements.

Embracing this method allows you to celebrate small victories along the way, which fuels motivation and keeps your spirit high. Each completed task, no matter how minor, brings you one step closer to your larger goal. It's a reminder that greatness is built one brick at a time, through persistent effort and unwavering dedication.

So, from this point forward, approach your aspirations with the mindset of a bricklayer: patient, focused, faithful, and committed, and you'll construct the life you envision.

The Twelve Principles

This book is structured around twelve principles that have significantly impacted my life. Here are the principles:

1. Gratitude
2. Setting Goals
3. Daily Actions
4. Living in the Present
5. Life Scripts and Affirmations
6. Exercise
7. Joyful Activities
8. The Five Things List
9. Attitude

10. MMFI (Make Me Feel Important)
11. Focus
12. Acting As If

Each chapter delves into one of these principles, providing practical steps that are simple to implement along with personal anecdotes to illustrate their importance. These principles are designed to be implemented gradually, one at a time, to create lasting change without any short-term overwhelm (or long term for that matter).

Moving Forward

Are you ready? It's time to get uncomfortable! I've discovered that stepping out of your comfort zone brings you into the learning zone, which is where your awareness expands and you gain skills that move you closer to your dreams. Before you know it, your comfort zone will have grown tenfold, and what might seem uncomfortable today has become a new part of who you naturally are. That might sound crazy, but it's true—I've definitely put this to the test, and so did my father along with the millions of people who followed his guidance.

As you begin applying the steps in this book, remember that success is not about overnight transformations. It's about putting forth consistent effort, being patient, and maintaining a positive attitude. Transformations could happen overnight—it's certainly possible—but that's not the point, nor the goal. By implementing the principles in this book, you will see gradual but profound changes in your life. These changes will not only benefit you but will also positively impact those around you.

When planting seeds in your garden, a lot of magic is happening below the surface before you ever see something sprout above ground. Transfer this awareness to everything we do together throughout this book, and trust the process knowing that your harvest is imminent.

I aim to inspire and guide you to discover your true potential so you can live an authentic, fulfilling life. Together, right now, let's take the next step toward your dreams and build a life of joy, success, freedom, and purpose.

1

GRATITUDE

After a lifetime of watching people attempt to make massive transformations in their lives, some successfully and others not so much, one thing has become clear to me: Change must start with gratitude.

We have an enormous capacity for happiness, and making a gratitude practice part of how we operate sets the stage to tap into that capacity. Think of it as the foundation for all the growth and success you will experience in your life. Gratitude is the base you can return to; gratitude grounds you. This principle is all too often underestimated in terms of its value.

When we don't practice gratitude, we naturally default to worry, doubt, and concern, especially about the future. This happens because we lose focus on the positive around us and become disconnected from possibility.

Let's face it: It's easy to see the negative today. The twenty-four-hour news cycle seems to be completely focused on bad news. Much of television and social media is negative—filled with rants, complaints, and an endless amount of chatter about how bad situations are.

But here is the thing. We always have a choice. We can choose which direction we want to turn our attention. We can easily absorb what's negative by not thinking—perhaps these negative ideas even justify our own position in life.

We can choose to complain—that is easy and may even feel natural to do, since it is the way the world trends. But we cannot transform anything, least ourselves, out of living in negativity and by consuming more negativity. To create forward motion in our lives, we need to look for and change our focus to what is positive and good. And that starts with us. It starts with a decision to do something different. To not follow the masses. To lead our life based on a greater level of awareness and a new, profound understanding.

What I am talking about here is a new lens for looking at life. That lens is gratitude. This is about choosing to look for the good that's around us. It has been well documented in research studies that we are happier and more generous, sleep better, and enjoy healthier relationships when we habitually feel the emotion of gratitude. Often, what it takes is a simple—yet not always easy—reframing of our circumstances. Establishing a gratitude practice is the base on which other successes in our life will build.

What is a gratitude practice exactly? Well, an easy example is every morning, before getting out of bed—or throughout the day, especially any time you feel frustration coming on—listing a few things you're grateful for in that moment. They can be significant items, like your home or your family—or simple items, like your ability to breathe or the satisfying cup of coffee you're about to enjoy. Allowing yourself to consciously notice the good in your life from an authentic perspective in the moment will activate a healthy vibration from which to go about your day.

Instead of starting your day by tuning into the chaos waiting for you inside your smartphone or television, a gratitude practice gets you off on the right track—on a much better vibe. You start your day inside out, rather than outside in.

When we are grateful for what we have, no matter how much or little that may be, we will naturally and easily attract better people, things, and circumstances into our lives, which opens us up to a brighter and more fulfilling world. Developing the habit of a gratitude practice will improve your relationships, including your relationship with yourself. It sets the context for all your daily experiences.

Sometimes, people view gratitude as rather passive. You had some good fortune and are grateful for that—you were lucky. What I am talking about with this practice is a much more proactive, intentional, and sustaining concept. It is about actively participating in the act of being grateful.

Nothing bolsters our outlook on the world like a consistent connection to a gratitude practice. It is important to understand that gratitude can shift your mindset regardless of how you believe you are wired, and while a shift in mindset may not immediately change your circumstances, it can change your outlook on life, which ultimately will have an effect on your circumstances, often sooner rather than later.

Even if it's just an ordinary day, you can still choose to open yourself up to the good that surrounds you—there is always good. Often, I will be grateful for something as simple as a cup of coffee—how the warm coffee cup feels in my hands, and the smell of the coffee as I take my first sip. Involving my senses in this way connects me to the visceral experience, which has positive effects below the surface of my mind and body chemistry. I am also creating a memory, and doing this will act as a trigger so that every time I have a hot drink in my hand, it will bring me back to this experience, automatically activating me to tap into that feeling of gratitude.

People may sneer at those who look at life through rose-colored glasses, but it takes a special person to look at life this way—and we certainly live a more joy-filled life than those doing the sneering. Choosing to always look for and focus on the good is a disciplined behavior.

I'm not saying that you'll never again see anything bad or that bad events aren't going to happen—we're not immune from adversity—but when we choose to find good, even in the adverse moments, we are putting less energy into what is bad and preventing it from consuming us. It is a better way to live—much better than walking around like a sourpuss, noticing and complaining about everything. Who wants to be around that? And really, who wants to *be* like that?

Here is the beautiful part: *You* get to decide how you want to show up in life. *You* decide how you will treat others and how you will treat yourself. *You* are the driver of your life. Someone else may have taught you how you've been behaving previously, but as of right here, right now, today, with this heightened awareness—YOU'RE IN CHARGE. Don't ever forget that.

I'm fortunate that being grateful has always been easy for me. I am so programmed not to give energy to the negative that even the thought of living this way makes me want to run in the other direction.

This way of being goes back to when I was a child. If my father wasn't on the road, he would tuck me into bed at night. I'll never forget the way I felt when Dad would come to tuck me in; he'd put his hand on my chest to create a physical connection, and we'd start talking about the day. He would talk about all the good events that happened that day and all the things he was grateful for. He would also ask me how my day had been and what I was grateful for.

If something bad had happened, we'd talk about it. However, he steered me away from focusing on the negative; he would gently guide me to look for the good. We'd then discuss what I'd learned from the negative experience. Dad was teaching me the healthy habit of finding the good even in the bad.

Our bedtime practice started when I was very young. It became so programmed in my adolescent mind that thinking this way quickly became a part of who I was, so I have always looked at everything with gratitude. If you're a parent, I highly recommend starting this practice with your little ones—even if your little ones aren't that little any longer. It's never too late.

That said, I certainly have had bad things happen to me—we all have. Did I get over them immediately? No, not always. Sometimes, I would wallow in that pain for a little bit. But, fairly quickly, I would recognize what I was doing, and I would realize that my attitude and focus on the negative event was not getting me anywhere. Then, instead, I would consciously switch my thoughts to focusing on the good and looking for the upside—and the lesson I'd learned. I'd ask myself how I could become better because of it. And then I'd express gratitude for the experience.

Practicing gratitude is not always easy, especially in the beginning when you start. But with repetition, you will more easily see the good all around you no matter what. It's often been said that the person who looks for the good in the world sees a world of good; the person who looks for the bad in the world sees a world of bad. This is a simple concept that I think you'll agree carries a lot of weight.

Gratitude—giving, receiving, and experiencing it—has an energy, and that vibration will cause a ripple effect in and around you. Scientifically, on the scale of emotional vibration, gratitude is measured to be among one of the highest emotions you can feel. You and the people around you are affected by whatever energy you are putting out, and the energy that comes from a grateful heart is a high-vibration energy.

This is not merely a cute philosophy. This is physics that today's technology can measure. Living your life this way, with this awareness and way of being, will give your life more meaning and motivation. You will be more resilient to the lumps and bumps of being human, and bounce back with greater strength from even your biggest challenges.

The Gratitude Journal

I have a gratitude journal on my desk. Every morning, I write inside about the good in my life. I'm very specific. Instead of saying, "I'm grateful for my family," I say, "I'm grateful for my loving son who always makes me laugh." Writing it out sets up my day in a positive way and helps me appreciate what is already in my life in very tangible, "feelable" way.

This is the way I personally practice gratitude; however, I'm not going to tell you how to keep your own journal. I believe we are each unique, and we must find what works for us—what resonates with our heart and soul. I like to write in complete sentences using words that express my emotions. Perhaps making bullet points works better for someone else. This is part of understanding who you are. You can try different ways of expressing gratitude, like trying on different pairs of shoes, until you find the one that feels the best for you. I can't overstate this—feeling is the most important part.

Personally, for events that have already happened or are happening currently, I write something like: "I am grateful that X is happening in my life." I also express gratitude for all the good that is coming my way in the future, and do so using the same present-tense sentence structure, even though it may not have come to fruition just yet.

Expressing gratitude for my future sets up an expectation that more good is coming my way. "I'm so grateful that X is coming to me." By doing that, I feel the gratitude, I'm in harmony with it, and it will come into my life. When? Who knows! But I am open to receiving it; I have set up an expectation in my mind and made a connection by writing it out, and that's been a game changer for me.

Dad had a license plate on his car that said, "EXPECT." That's what this is. It's a way of expecting good to come into your life. And not from an ego-centric perspective but rather from a higher awareness perspective that this is how life and the Universe works.

Again, there isn't a right or wrong way to do journaling. The key is to get something to write in that you can leave on your desk or by your bedside, where you see it every day, that triggers positive vibes.

In doing your gratitude practice consistently, some days will seem harder than others. Some days, we might not be feeling particularly grateful. But if we can habitually force ourselves to open that page, think about what we're grateful for, and write it down, even if it's just a few simple notations, this process itself will change our perspective. Doing this will help create a shift in mental state and emotional vibration, and ease negative, angry, and sad feelings if we're feeling low, shortening the period of negativity that could otherwise keep us paralyzed and do real damage.

As I mentioned in the introduction, like the tide, the world ebbs and flows, and gratitude is a state of mind—an attitude that we choose to live by regardless of our day-to-day circumstances because it's the nature of life to experience ups and downs. When we resume being in a grateful state of mind coming out of the low points, our physiology and world around us responds in tone and we resume attracting better into our lives.

In all the seminars and events I have attended in my lifetime to date, there has always been a lot of talk about gratitude journals and taking time each morning to write out what you're grateful for. The funny thing is that most people hear this message but never put it into practice.

My dad always started his day with a journal and took some quiet time in the morning to reflect and write out everything he was grateful for. When he finished writing, he would sit quietly and ask for some divine guidance for the day. Starting his day this way set him up for the good he desired and deserved. Because of his example, I live this way, too, and the positive effects are obvious.

If you are looking for a simple tool to help you live your life with a calm, confident heart and energy, you need to start a gratitude journal right now. *Need* is a strong word, and trust me, I use it with intention and certainty for you.

Viewing the world through the lens of gratitude will open you up to opportunities you quite likely may have missed before. You will view life with a new and softer perspective. You and I are like magnets, and we will attract more of what we put out in the world. We get to choose what we want that to be.

You may be at a point where something bad has happened to you: bankruptcy, divorce, abuse, trauma, depression, crime, theft, you name it. We've all been there at one point or another. When you find yourself in life's challenging moments, it may seem extremely difficult to see the good or feel gratitude in a meaningful way.

I am not a psychologist, and I won't have the answer for everybody. But I would offer that you don't need to be grateful for that bad thing: Some of these occurrences are frankly terrible, and there's nothing innate about them to be grateful for. But even in these awful moments, we can choose to shift our thinking around that event and be grateful, not for the event itself, but for what we have learned from it and how we can become stronger because of it.

It may take a while before you see anything good, but when we can change our perspective, even on terrible events, we can loosen the emotional hold it may have on us and dull the sharp edges. We can convert a potential lifetime of trauma to, instead, only last a few days or weeks, and we can recycle that experience into something positive that serves us and others. Many people who have gone through some of the worst experiences imaginable have bounced back to help millions of people by sharing what they learned and how to prevent or overcome such experiences.

Another point is this: Don't let bad fortune form your identity. That may be easier said than done in some situations, but as I said earlier, while we cannot change some events, we can change our perspective about them. Whatever's happened has happened. What's done is done. If you are tired of hearing yourself complain, it is likely that others are, too, and it's time to look for the good and move on instead of dragging along the baggage of the past with you into the present.

When an emotion from a negative event lasts more than a few hours, it becomes a mood. When the negative emotion lasts more than a few days, it becomes a temperament. And when it lasts years, it becomes a personality trait. Stop letting the past form who you are in the present. Limit its impact to a temporary mood, and return as soon as possible to your innate, divine nature.

Make a shift, even if initially just for five minutes, and give yourself a break. Look within your current space and surroundings and find something beautiful. It is natural to take the most meaningful parts of our lives for granted, and we're often blind to the beauty around us right now, especially when it's muddied with a bad mood, temperament, or personality.

As an exercise in shifting your attitude and awareness, imagine if the things currently in your life were taken away. For example, imagine waking up tomorrow without the people in your life that you are closest to. How would this absence make you feel? Linger there for a moment. This will provide you with a profound sense of gratitude for what has become your every day. If you've ever gone through the experience of having lost a loved one, let that experience be a reminder to cherish what you have for as long as you get to enjoy it.

When you form the habit of looking for and acknowledging the good in your life and start changing your focus to that rather than on the negative, you will start to look at life a little differently (or a lot) and you will tune into a new you: your best self. Your view might not change overnight, but with this practice every day, you will form this beautiful habit that can become a tool for pulling yourself out of a negative lifestyle.

Don't let bad fortune form a part of your identity.

History is history, and as I said, you can't change what's been done. History has brought us to where we are now. We wouldn't be here without that history, good or bad. We don't need to whitewash the bad things that are in our personal history and the history of the world. But we can look for the good—what we've learned from it. Even if we notice we've been operating from a negative personality for the past several years. How can we now begin to improve as a result? Maybe in some situations, we haven't started the improvements yet, but the potential is there, now.

As the great Wayne Dyer said, "Change the way you look at things, and the things you look at will change. How people treat you is their karma; how you react is yours." We might be unable to change the world right now or how everybody else looks at it. Even so, we can change how we look at that world. We can ask, How can I be better because of this? How can I look for the good here?

I've been fortunate enough to have some superior models of gratitude in my life. The person who first comes to my mind is the late Lloyd Conant, of Nightingale Conant Corporation, the personal development company. I knew Lloyd when I was a young boy. He was like a grandfather figure to me. My memory of him is of an incredibly kind man. He was good to my father, and Dad always spoke highly of him. He encouraged me to look at everything as gifts—good and bad. He taught me that all my experiences may not feel good, but they all were necessary to who I was becoming.

As I've already emphasized, what I'm spelling out here is not one great, decisive act. People sometimes approach self-development that way, and it usually doesn't work. Changing your life for the better is not a one-time event that sticks forever, like a caterpillar transforming into a butterfly. A better analogy is a weak person who uses a regular weightlifting regimen to gain a powerful, muscular physique. If that routine is not sustained, that person will return to their original physique. Adding a gratitude practice into your life is like a strength training routine for your heart, mind, and soul. Its effects domino into every facet of your life.

Changing your life for the better is not a one-time event.

With any of the practices you're adopting in this book, you need to do the practice every day; that's where the value is for you. By doing them every day, you turn the practices into habits, and eventually, you do them automatically. The activities become your way of being—they're not just something you do, but rather they become a part of who you are. You don't have to think about breathing, you just do it. Likewise, you won't have to think about being grateful any longer, you'll just be it.

When incorporating these practices into your daily life, think of it this way. The person who goes to the gym and works out regularly and consistently will not have that buff body in one day. They could work out intensely for two weeks, and, even then, they will hardly even see any difference. But we know that if this person continues every single day, two or three months from now, they will see a difference.

The same is true with all the practices I'm discussing in this book. We might not see a change immediately, but in time, when we look back and connect the dots, we will be shocked at how far we have come and so proud of ourselves for staying the course.

It's probably not going to be easy, and, yes, you'll forget a day or two. Don't worry about that. Instead, recommit to your practice and keep going. It is like that Chinese proverb: "The best time to plant a tree was twenty years ago. The second best time is now." Don't let stumbling stop you from continuing. When you do miss a day, don't beat yourself up. Just start again. Life gets a lot easier when we treat ourselves with grace and compassion.

I've highlighted that this book is about simple steps, and they are simple when you choose to keep it that way. If we want to make it difficult, we can do that by overthinking and not taking action. It's a matter of choice and commitment to change. Personally, I've always decided to choose easy. Easy just feels better to me. How about for you?

Fixed on the Best

There's a poignant quote from Wallace D. Wattles, who wrote a classic inspirational book, *The Science of Getting Rich*, in the early twentieth century. He said, "The grateful mind is constantly fixed upon the best. Therefore, it tends to become the best. It takes the form or character of the best and will receive the best."

This quote points to an important aspect of gratitude: Maintaining a positive mental attitude and expressing gratitude for what you have, while cultivating a forward-thinking attitude that expects and imagines a prosperous future, is how you create change. These are critical components of attracting wealth and success in life.

It's about being happy with what we've got while knowing our future is bright and bringing something even better. Gratitude unblocks us from some of the negative energy that we can find ourselves in. When we're fed nonsense all the time, from the media or sometimes from people close to us, we can fall into their rabbit hole if we are not guarding our minds. A daily gratitude practice will help to keep us on a positive track and guard us from any potentially long-lasting effects of negativity.

Appreciating Where You Are

Another important technique is appreciating where we are right now. For me, I love nature, and I like to sit outside and watch and listen to what's around me. Doing this quickly gets me into a significant state of gratitude. When I'm in the woods, out on the water, looking for animals, or just enjoying my environment, whatever that is, I feel at peace. Nature takes me out of my thinking mind and into my feeling heart.

It's good practice to find a place where you can sit, look around, and be thankful for where you are. Being outdoors can fill us with a sense of awe that deepens our gratitude for life itself. This happens when we can take ourselves out of our heads and instead focus on the incredible beauty that surrounds us. Isn't it incredible what's all around us, both natural and man-made?

Nature is one catalyst, but you can practice appreciating where you are anytime and anywhere. Let's say you are in a restaurant and get good service. In addition to giving a tip, you can look that person in the eye and express how grateful you are.

If somebody has touched your life in a positive way, through service or any other way, it's important to let them know what they've done for you and how it's made you feel. Certainly, expressing your thoughts will make you feel good to share that with them. Besides, you never know what that message can do for the person you're sharing it with. You can alter somebody's day just by doing that. Sharing your gratitude with others opens you energetically to attract better into your life—and it's a win-win proposition.

Some people like to send handwritten thank-you notes to others. Although it's becoming a lost art in this digital age, a note can be a thoughtful practice. I must admit that this is not a practice I do myself, but my wife, Cory, does. She's always looking for nice paper and envelopes, and she is forever sending handwritten notes to people. I love watching her do that.

You can impact someone's life with a simple message of thanks, whether verbal, written, or digital. I know the person she's sending the note to will feel special, but I also know what it does for Cory to write that note. It's a gift for the giver as well as the gifted.

There's one major impediment to gratitude that I think everyone needs to recognize. It can be particularly acute in the age of social media where people constantly post pictures of themselves and their beautiful cars, homes, and vacations, but it has been present for as long as anyone can remember. It's comparison.

If you think about it, comparison leads to what used to be called one of the seven deadly sins: envy. Among whatever else envy is or might be, it certainly can be a ruthless killer of gratitude.

To prevent this problem, it's important to start by refusing to compare ourselves to anybody. In the first place, it's hard to know what's real and what's not anymore (I'm sure you've seen some of those social media vs. real-life memes); but besides that, this life is not a race or a competition, and it's time we stop treating it like it is.

Refuse to compare yourself to anybody else.

When you see someone who has something that you think is better than what you have, just think, "Well, good for them. That's great," and go back to appreciating where you are. Stay in your lane and work on you. Let the possibilities inspire you instead of allowing a perceived lack bring you down.

If we get into the comparison game, we are going down a bad path. If we see somebody with something we perceive as better, it will make us feel less. That's not a good place to be. It's much more productive to appreciate that we are where we are because of what we've done. If we want to be in a better place, we can ask, What can I do today to be better than who I was yesterday?

Eventually, we will get to where we want to be if we can live in gratitude for where we are and where we're going. Your job should be working on being the best version of you. When you focus on that, your life will become what you want it to be.

And do not fall into the trap of thinking someone who is experiencing abundance doesn't deserve it because they didn't work hard for it or because someone gave it to them. Truthfully, it's none of your business how they got what they have. You are much better served to focus on what's going on in your own life, on what you want for yourself, and then get busy attracting it. Anything else is a waste of your valuable time and energy. So far as we know, we only get one life, so don't squander it.

You are capable of choosing the best version of yourself right now. You can do this in dealing with your wife, husband, or partner, with your kids, your parents, your job, your business, or a task that you're involved in. When you can be the best version of yourself in this moment, you are actively and proactively creating change.

Our "best" will vary from day to day. I suggest you always strive to be better than you were yesterday, but don't beat yourself up if your performance today is not quite up to par. Remember the ebb and flow, and commit to doing your best again tomorrow.

Having this foundation of a positive focus, coupled with gratitude, strengthens your capacity to navigate life. And it amplifies the good that is already present. Committing to a consistent gratitude practice will put you on the path to fulfilling the potential that lies within you. Now, exercise this awareness—what's one thing you are grateful for right now?

Key Points

- Understand that gratitude is the base from which all success in your life will grow.
- Looking for the good in life will always open you up to better.
- Start a gratitude journal. Every morning, write about all that you are grateful for.
- Gratitude will help you see opportunities that you may have missed and elevate your vibration.
- Don't compare yourself to anyone else.

2

SET A GOAL

I can vividly remember when my journey of setting goals originally began. It was my fifteenth birthday, and just thinking about it still brings a smile to my face.

Dad handed me a small wrapped box. I've always been good at guessing gifts, but this one had me stumped. It was small, and I could feel something heavy inside that moved around freely. I had no idea what I was about to open. As I peeled off the wrapping, a plain box was revealed, offering no clues. When I finally opened the box, I found a small toy car inside. My first thought was, Why am I getting a toy car at fifteen? But then I noticed a note tucked beneath it.

That note was a defining moment in my life, changing how I approached the world. It simply read: *Brian, one year from now I will match every dollar you save. It can be used toward the purchase of a car.*

For me as a teenager, this was an exhilarating idea. The thought of having my own car represented a freedom unlike anything I had experienced before. For the first time, I set a goal that pushed me to do things I had never done. I started visiting car lots, imagining myself behind the wheel of my own vehicle. That small gift ignited a spark in me that motivated my teenage self to think bigger.

I began considering how I could start earning and saving money. The first step was applying for part-time work, and, soon enough, I secured a job at a local ice cream parlor. Looking back, it makes me laugh—my pay was $1.95 an hour.

I took every shift I could get after school and on weekends. I also began thinking of other ways to boost my savings. I canvassed the neighborhood, offering to mow lawns in the summer and shovel snow in the winter. Mowing lawns was easy; it was warm and enjoyable. Shoveling snow, on the other hand, was cold, windy, and just plain nasty. But I kept at it because, for the first time, I had a goal that truly motivated me to push through discomfort.

I might have made $5 for each driveway I cleared in the winter or lawn I mowed in the summer, but it all added up. I even cut back on going to the movies with friends to save more money. Imagining myself driving my own car made me willing to sacrifice short-term pleasures for a bigger reward.

This was the first time in my life that I was truly driven by a goal. The experience taught me lessons that have stayed with me ever since. Through this process, my father inspired me to step out of my comfort zone and do more. It was thrilling. To this day, I lean on that experience when I'm chasing big dreams, knowing that with dedication and hard work, I will achieve what I set out to do.

A year later, I had saved up a sizable sum for a teenager. Dad matched what I had earned, and I was able to purchase a wonderful car that holds a special place in my memory. The car wasn't just a mode of transportation; it was a symbol of my hard work and determination. But the true reward was what I learned along the way.

I discovered what I was capable of achieving. I learned the value of hard work and the importance of having a goal to strive for. My days were filled with intention and clarity. It was a priceless lesson in the power of setting and pursuing goals, rather than just drifting through life.

I can still remember the smell of that car and the immense pride I felt every time I drove it. And that little toy car that came in the box? I still have it! It serves as a constant reminder of the valuable lessons I learned at a young age—lessons that continue to shape my life decades later.

What Is a Goal?

During all the years that my father taught goal setting, he never deviated from what he called the perfect definition of success in life. It came from his mentor Earl Nightingale.

Earl defined success as the progressive realization of a worthy ideal. This worthy ideal is the goal a person sets for themselves.

The real purpose in life is not to acquire anything or to get anywhere. The real purpose in life is to grow. The thing you must endeavor to discover is what you want: what you enjoy—then you work to get it. To get it, you must grow. Develop your talent and ability—provide more service—grow! The real gift is the growth; the getting of the thing is a bonus.

A way I like to think of this is like a road trip. I have my map, I know where I am starting, I know where I am going, and I am going to be very happy when I get there. I am going to look around, enjoy where I am, and have a few good meals, but the real adventure is going to be all the places I stopped along the way. The destination is a result of the progressive realization. And, as you've likely heard it said before, the joy is in the journey.

Now, that is a really simple way to think of this, but it does explain what my father and Earl are saying here. A goal keeps you on track because you know where you are going; it is the engine that drives you to your dreams. Success inevitably happens along the way when you are purposefully working toward something that is worthy.

Think about the times in your life when you have been working toward something. Working toward a

worthy goal is how I was raised. Dad was always helping me to stretch and to define what I wanted.

Set a Goal

Imagine asking anyone on the street about a goal they
have. Most people would give you a blank look or
scramble for a quick answer. The truth is, very few of
us have set a clear goal that genuinely inspires us to
our core and makes us want to jump out of bed every
morning. And without a big, inspiring goal, we're just
going through the motions of life. Another famous quote
from Earl Nightingale is, "Most people tiptoe their way
through life, hoping to make it safely to death." Boy,
isn't that the truth. And they don't even realize this is
what they're doing.

Without a big goal, we're not going to be inspired
to do anything differently over the long haul. We might
want and wish for a better life, but we never acquire
any real knowledge about how to get there or take any
real action toward that end. Again, the real purpose in
life is to grow.

When we are not guided by a personal or professional goal, it is easy to get off track, or never get onto
any particular track with intention in the first place.
The demands of people, places, circumstances, and life
by default dominate our day, and we mindlessly find
ourselves tending to daily trivia.

My father taught me that when we set a big goal
that is not easy to achieve—but rather, one that inspires

us, that we have no idea how to accomplish initially—
we create change within ourselves because the pursuit
of that goal causes us to step out and do things that we
would not normally do. Our success is what happens
along the journey toward our goal—that is our growth.
We're naturally learning along the way because of the
actions we are taking. In doing so, we are fulfilling our
life purpose.

When we don't have a goal, we're working without direction, which makes us more susceptible to the
whims of what is happening around us. It takes the
strength of a worthy goal that we can feel on an emotional level to keep what is happening outside of us
from taking us off track or quite frankly from making
us potentially miserable or uninspired.

What I have learned is that I can better control my
thoughts and actions when I'm consciously and intentionally working toward something. The goal keeps me
from simply bouncing along from day to day without
direction, because I can make yes and no decisions
about what I'm doing, only working in harmony on
tasks that are related to where I'm going.

With a goal guiding me, I have order, and I stay
focused on my destination. I don't worry about my
next steps because they always reveal themselves
along the way, just like when I follow my GPS on a
road trip, so I only focus on the next one or two steps
in front of me.

Right this moment I have a powerful goal that keeps
me going every day. I don't know all the steps to get-

ting there, but I'm enjoying the journey and trusting one step will lead to the next—and ultimately, the final destination.

Robert Heinlein had a great statement: "In the absence of clearly defined goals, we become strangely loyal to performing daily trivia until ultimately we become enslaved by it." You see, living without a goal is a sure way to expend energy and other resources without getting results. And this is how most people live, drifting along each day like a ship that's lost at sea.

How do you set a goal?

Start thinking about what inspires you. Your motivating goal could be to run a marathon, start a business, learn a new language, write a book, travel the world, or even start a charity. The key is to select a goal that truly drives you without worrying about others' opinions, and without worrying about whether you already know how to do it.

Years ago, in the eighties, my father hosted what he called the Goal Achiever Seminar. This seminar was a game changer for me. It provided the tools and mindset I needed to set and achieve my goals. I always left those sessions with my productivity soaring.

Here's the simple but powerful approach he taught: Take a piece of paper and imagine you have a magic wand. What would you wish for in your life? Write down everything you desire, no matter how outlandish it seems. Don't think about how you'll achieve it or whether it's possible—just list your dreams as if anything were possible.

If you had that magic wand, what would you write down? For the next week or so, keep this exercise up daily. Over the next few days, you might notice one or two goals consistently standing out. Focus on those. As you continue, you'll refine and clarify your list, crossing off what no longer resonates.

Never worry about how you'll achieve these goals. If it's a truly compelling goal, you won't see the path to achieving it yet. However, if you're genuinely committed, you'll find a way to make progress every day. That's how you know you've chosen a worthwhile goal—you're excited, maybe a bit scared, but absolutely committed, even without a clear path forward. Start with one step at a time and build from there, like constructing that brick house I talked about earlier: brick by brick, you'll attract it.

While setting goals is the start, goal setting and achieving is more than a mere exercise. It's much more than simply scribbling down a few tasks you want to achieve without a concrete plan. If you've ever done this and found you didn't get anywhere, it's because you didn't establish a routine of daily habits that support your progression forward. When you initially set your goals, you don't need anything other than your burning desire to get going on them; but as you progress forward, you must begin to craft your plans, step by step, brick by brick.

The Journal of Goals

Here's a technique I use to stay focused on my goals. I keep two journals on my desk, one for gratitude, which I already discussed in the previous chapter, and one for goal setting.

In the gratitude journal, I write down what I'm grateful for each day, which helps me maintain a positive mindset. In the goal-setting journal, I write down my goal in this form: "I am so happy and grateful now that [goal]."

This was a practice I learned from my father. Like me, he was an early riser, and one of his first actions in the morning after gratitude was to write out his goals. His routine included gratitude, goal writing, asking for divine guidance for the day, reflection on what is and what's to come, and studying personal development materials. He was always striving to improve himself and this routine set him up for success in a big way for over sixty years, right up until his final days on earth.

I adopted his approach with open arms. Every day, I write a succinct and brief five-line statement of my goal. This practice reinforces my goal in my mind and directs my focus and energy. By writing it out, I'm reinforcing the goal in my mind, but more importantly, I'm putting my focus and attention onto it, which lingers throughout the rest of the day on both the conscious and subconscious levels.

This daily morning exercise is about maintaining a focused energy on something specific—something that causes growth. We must use whatever tools work for us to stay on track. As long as we remain focused on our goal, we'll achieve it. That's a fact.

Typically, achieving a big goal takes time. No significant goal is reached overnight, but if it's inspiring enough, the pursuit of the goal will push us to take actions we wouldn't normally take, and we won't be concerned with the amount of time it may take to manifest. This goal achievement process fosters personal growth and reveals potential within us that we very likely may never have realized without it.

You'll observe that when you start pursuing your bigger goals, the people around you will notice a change. They'll see a difference in you, and that can be both positive and negative (from their perspective).

When you push yourself to achieve more, you'll encounter support from some people, while others may resist. Understand this: People don't resist change itself, they resist being changed. And as you grow, you're altering the dynamics of your relationships beyond the direct control of the other people, which can be unsettling for those who prefer staying in their comfort zones rather than stepping into the growth zone.

Unfortunately, dare I say, most people resist and want to stay comfortable. I suggest you move forward anyway, and know that in time, they could possibly come around as they start to feel inspired by your progress. However, if they don't, know that's their choice, and it's their responsibility to deal with their own moods, temperaments, and personality traits.

You do you, and let them do them. If they do support you, recognize them as someone special in your life, and let them know how grateful you are for that.

Here's an important point: Only share your goals and discuss progress and challenges with those who genuinely support you. In the early stages of goal setting, you need all the encouragement you can get. If you broadcast your goals to just anyone, you open yourself up to a flood of opinions that could derail you, because by default, we value the opinion of others and often forget it's just an opinion based upon their own limited perception. Remember, they can't see what you see in terms of your potential. You don't need that kind of negativity. Be selective about who you confide in regarding your goals, and remember that any doubt or negativity is their stuff, their baggage—it's not yours.

Share your goal only with people who will support you.

Sometimes, those closest to you might not be supportive, and that's okay. You don't have to share your aspirations with them. Love them anyway and stay the course in the direction of your dreams.

Focus on finding a supportive community or mentor who can help you stay motivated and on track, even when others doubt your goals. You are your only problem, and you are your only solution. It's up to you to surround yourself with positive influences and find them if they're not originally present in your life. Trust me: They are out there, and they're waiting for you.

The Matrixx

Around three times a year, in my father's personal development organization, we held a five-day seminar in Toronto called The Matrixx. It was one of my favorite seminars to participate in. We organized up to a hundred participants into groups of eight at roundtables. The focus was on helping each person clarify their goals.

On the first day, many participants looked confused, like deer in headlights. As the week progressed and each exercise built upon the last, we could feel the excitement and clarity grow at each table and in the entire room as a whole.

I've come to understand that crafting a clear, concise statement of your goal can be a real struggle for many, because it's not something they were ever taught how to do before they started their work with us. Getting clear about your goal is crucial, but it can be challenging to achieve, especially in the beginning. It may take some time, and that's normal—so give yourself some slack, but don't neglect it.

Once you've homed in on a clear vision of what you're pursuing, you should be able to express it in a brief statement of two or three sentences, no more than five. This statement should be so straightforward that even a stranger could understand your goal without any confusion and without the need to hear a long background story.

During the Matrixx goal exercises, I often saw participants struggling with conciseness. Many of their statements were vague, like, I want to be successful, or I want to be happy.

We'd review their statements and ask, What exactly are you trying to achieve? If they couldn't answer, we'd pose questions to help clarify their goals both in their minds and on paper. Our mission was to get them to articulate their objectives in a clear and concise manner so everyone at the table would understand their precise intent.

The precision is how you know you've nailed it. Once you've crafted that clear statement, it's time to write down your goal every day in your journal. This isn't just about repetition; it's about reinforcing your commitment and belief in your goal.

At first, you might not fully believe in your goal or in your ability to achieve it, but as long as you're inspired, keep writing it out anyway. This daily practice puts you in the driver's seat of your journey, empowering you to stay focused and committed, and after a bit of time, you'll start to feel a clear affinity with your goal.

There's a notion that if we write something often enough, even if it's not true, we'll eventually start to believe it. This principle applies here as well. Even if you don't fully believe in your goal at first, consistent daily writing in the present tense will help you start to embrace its possibility—meaning you begin to see it as something that could actually happen; it's no longer just a distant dream.

You need to believe in yourself and in your goal, but here's the thing about beliefs: A belief is just a thought that you keep thinking. When you start writing and thinking about your goal, you may not believe it yet; but the repetition of thinking about it and writing it out will cement the belief over time, and once the belief is firm, it becomes destiny. Again, this is not just a cute idea; this is physics, backed by neuroscience and other mechanisms for measurement.

As I've mentioned, obstacles will arise—fear, criticism from naysayers, and procrastination, to name just a few. There will be days when you're emotionally drained and lack the motivation to continue. Undoubtedly, there will be moments that test your resolve. However, the way you deal with these obstacles is not a matter of chance but a conscious choice.

To deal with these obstacles, first, you must reaffirm the value and purpose of your goals and strengthen your belief in your ability to achieve them. Second, you must recognize that these challenges are not failures, but necessary parts of the journey. Denzel Washington famously talks about "failing forward," and this is a phenomenal analogy for you to embrace.

When you find your commitment wavering, it's crucial to understand the thoughts clouding your mind and where they're coming from. Ask yourself, What can I do right now that might not yield significant results but will help me regain my focus? It might be something as simple as writing down your intention. Then, take a break for the day; don't force things. And don't let discouragement take over.

Be kind to yourself, and when you're ready, get back on track by expressing gratitude and revisiting your goal. Sometimes, you just need a short period of time to go for a walk, listen to music, pet your cat or dog, or do something else that shifts you back into a more positive vibration to pick back up where you left off.

I remember when I was writing my first book, *My Father Knew the Secret*, and I would hit a point of discouragement. At that moment, I wasn't sure how to proceed or what message to convey. I was grieving the recent loss of my father and felt lost and at times paralyzed.

My wife, Cory, suggested a simple approach: "Brian, just write five hundred words each day. It's not much. Even if you're not in the mood, write those five hundred words, then do something else you enjoy, like kayaking or fishing."

"Okay," I said, "I can do that."

During these points of discouragement, I was allowing myself to feel overwhelmed by the bigness of my goal of a finished book. I was looking at the big thing, and I wasn't focused on the little things I could do. The next day, I started with five hundred words. Some days, I wrote more because I was in the flow. On other days, I stuck to the lower word count and then enjoyed a break.

Over a few months, I amassed a substantial amount of content. I reached my larger goal almost effortlessly by focusing on the immediate, manageable task, and I'm grateful to Cory for inspiring me to stop waiting for that big thing!

I had a similar experience building the email list for my father's company, which grew to well over one million subscribers. When I began, it was the early 2000s and there were no email list-building services like there are today. I started off emailing every person one by one. It was a challenging task, and my learning curve was steep. But I was committed because I knew the list would benefit the company and honor my father's mission. If I had known at the time all that I would have to do to create it, I probably wouldn't have done it.

Sometimes, ignorance is an advantage.

Despite the challenges, I remained committed to building the list for my father's company. Each day, I put in the work, and, gradually, I put the systems in place. I was determined to find better ways of assembling the emails, and, as a result, improvement happened rapidly. My commitment to the outcome helped me navigate obstacles and find solutions along the way. Even when setbacks occurred, I learned from each one and advanced further.

Many people have ambitious goals and spend time planning and strategizing, yet they often hesitate to take action. They wait for the perfect moment, the ideal plan, or the perfect conditions—aka "that big thing."

However, most often, taking imperfect action is the most effective approach.

It's through these imperfect steps that we learn and make progress, feeling empowered by our ability to adapt and grow. Remember, fail forward. Mistakes and imperfections are part of the journey, but if we keep moving forward, we will eventually reach our destination.

Inaction, on the other hand, leads to nothing. Two steps forward and one step back is way better than no steps forward.

Occasionally, we set a goal with a specific deadline, only to find that the date passes without achieving it. When this happens, it's important not to get discouraged by missing the timeline. Setting a date is simply a target; it can be a great thing to do, but we must remember that when we set a target date, we are just guessing, and it's okay if we need to adjust the date as we go along. The key is that we're making progress, creating change, and growing. That's what actually matters—that's the real success. The progressive realization of the worthy ideal.

The Million-Dollar Yacht

Dad hosted many seminars every year, and there was one couple in particular who attended nearly every one of them, year after year. They were always present, sitting at the front with their notebooks ready. Even if they'd heard a particular lesson in the past, they listened as if it was their first seminar, which is an attitude I suggest you adopt as well.

This couple already ran a very successful air-conditioning company in the southern United States but knew they hadn't reached their full potential. They were eager to learn about setting and achieving bigger and better goals.

The husband had decided he wanted a million-dollar yacht, which was a personal goal far beyond anything they had ever pursued. My father told him, "You don't need to know every detail right now. Just make the decision. If that's what you sincerely want and that goal inspires you, commit to it, and you'll figure out the rest."

The business owner took that advice to heart. He made the decision and wrote about how it would feel to sail with his family and friends on his grand yacht. This newfound inspiration drove him to take actions in his business he hadn't considered before. He stepped back from his usual business model and began thinking more creatively, which allowed him to serve more customers and hire more employees. As he was driven by his goal, he began to see new opportunities and took actions that changed his daily routine.

I don't remember the exact timeline, but it wasn't long before he acquired that yacht. He sailed from Louisiana to Florida, where I was living at the time, and I met him in the bay. When he dropped anchor, I saw the yacht he had envisioned, and it was appropriately named *Persistence*. It was an impressive sight, and he beamed with pride at his accomplishment, inspiring those around him with his determination and success. He shared that setting this goal had shifted his perspective on his business, leading to significant improvements.

While the yacht was a wonderful reward, the real impact was on his business, his employees, and his customers. The focus on something inspiring prompted him to approach his work differently; he thought outside of the box he'd been operating in, and it benefited him and the people he served.

So let me ask you, "What's your yacht?"

A couple of years later, I received a call from this couple. It was fun catching up and discussing their journey using our goal-setting materials. They had started a small business in their garage, which grew into a multimillion-dollar enterprise through hard work and vision.

They continued to set and achieve bigger goals, staying excited and motivated. Eventually, they sold their company for a substantial sum and were set for life. Their success stemmed from the simple lessons they learned about goal setting and application, which left them with a deep sense of fulfillment and contentment.

Their business success was due to their ambitions and commitment to serving their community and employees. This mindset led to transformative changes in their lives and in the lives of those around them. When they sold the company, they generously gifted many of their key employees, enhancing their lives as well. Their commitment to being grateful and doing good continued to bring positive outcomes into their lives.

Using Deadlines

When it comes to goal setting, it's important to recognize that we all have unique ways of working, and you need to discover what works best for you for staying motivated and on track as you progress forward daily.

I've observed that some people thrive by focusing solely on the big vision—their grand goal drives them every single day. They keep that vision constantly in their minds, using it as their motivation. It doesn't feel overwhelming to them, and it's enough.

For others, setting smaller milestone deadlines can be incredibly helpful. Here's how the process works: Take your big goal and deconstruct it into smaller, manageable parts. Assign deadlines to these smaller pieces and concentrate on achieving them within those timeframes. Think of it like a cross-country road trip. You know your final destination, but each day's journey involves different stops and milestones along the way. You're still headed to your end goal, but your daily focus is on the immediate step at hand. My father called this "reducing things to the ridiculous."

Understanding how you work best is key.

Personally, I employ a blend of these approaches. I hold the big vision in my mind, but I also take consistent, manageable steps toward it. By doing this, I keep my eyes on the grand prize while ensuring I make daily progress without overwhelm.

I break down my large goals into bite-sized actions to avoid discouragement and maintain focus. Each morning, I write out my big goal to stay aligned with my ultimate destination, and I also have my next action step outlined.

Again, you've got to become aware of what works best for you. If you find that a big goal without a clear path of milestones feels overwhelming, break it down into steps—as many as you can see right now. Maybe you need to divide it into ten actionable steps—do that. Start with the first step, complete it, and then move on to the next. After you take the first step, you may find that the next step is different from what you outlined. Remain flexible and follow the gratitude-infused brick road.

Sometimes, people get caught up in creating a detailed, step-by-step plan, especially those with analytical minds. While planning is important, it can also become a trap. Planning without acting can lead to perpetual stagnation. I've seen many who overplan but never move forward, and they end up stuck in the same place as those who never set goals in the first place. Subconsciously, it may be that a fear of failure or fear of success is keeping them stuck at planning and preventing the all-important action-taking from ensuing.

I firmly believe that taking imperfect action as soon as you can is far better than taking no action at all, or waiting a long time to have the perfect plan before

Best Practices for Goal Setting

1. Decide what you want.
2. Write down your goal.
3. Set a target deadline for the goal, remaining flexible.
4. (Optional) List intermediate steps.
5. Take action every day to move toward your goal.

you act. Contrary to what your logical mind or people around you may be saying, you don't need to see the entire path right now to reach your destination. In fact, not knowing every detail might keep your inspiration alive and prevent you from getting bogged down by details that feel overwhelming. My earlier story about building the email list in my father's company is a great example of this.

You don't need to know the entire way in order to get there.

Returning to the essence of this book, it's essential to understand your core desires, but not wait for something big to make them manifest. Simply take one step at a time, and the path will unfold as you go. Over-planning often leads to inaction; whereas, setting clear milestone goals as far as you can currently see provides a clear initial direction and boosts your confidence.

So far, we've explored goal setting on an individual level, but the same principles apply to groups—whether it's business teams, sports squads, or even families.

Reflecting on my experiences with my father's company, I remember how impactful our team retreats were. About twelve or thirteen years ago, we took our decision-makers to Hawaii for a series of company retreats. We stayed at a stunning resort, where each morning was dedicated to brainstorming and strategizing on how to support one another's growth. The afternoons were reserved for enjoyable activities like whale watching or hiking.

These retreats allowed us to connect on a personal level. We understood each other's challenges and found ways to support one another. We built strong friendships while focusing on a shared big goal, such as increasing our market share by 20 percent. Beyond the overarching company objective, we set individual goals such as improving our sales techniques or enhancing our customer service that contributed to the larger vision, and we made sure each of these goals was personally inspiring. This approach was incredibly effective and led to substantial growth for the company.

Our success was rooted in a positive, collective mindset that valued and fostered individual creativity. Instead of having a single leader dictate the path, we formed a collaborative team, each person contributing uniquely toward our shared goal. This method isn't limited to business—it's equally valuable in family and other team dynamics. It makes each member feel integral to the team's success.

These retreats were the ideal example of team building and allowing each person to prosper and share their unique wisdom to help build something bigger for the company. We all felt invested in the outcome. Each person could do their part to help promote my father and his activities. Because of that process, my father became better known around the world, and he was able to reach a larger audience.

When working with an organization, it's crucial to ensure that each member feels like a valued part of something special, not just a cog in the machine. If you can make people feel significant and capable of contributing, your group will achieve its goals more swiftly and effectively—like a rowing team, each member propelling the craft in the same direction.

Digital Tools

In terms of goal setting, you can use a simple pen and paper or a journal, but there are also numerous digital tools available. Set reminders on your phone to keep your goal in view. The key is to find what works for you.

For me, hand-writing my goals each morning is a powerful practice. It creates a mind-body connection that typing doesn't (for me, anyway) and reinforces my focus and commitment. However, if digital does it for you, do that.

I learned this practice from my father, who encouraged me from a young age to set big goals and keep track of them daily. His consistent questioning, "What are you doing today to get closer to your goal?" was incredibly motivating. Find your own cheerleader—someone who inspires you and helps you stay on track. Their encouragement can be a powerful motivator in your journey toward achieving your goals. And in your moments of self-doubt, you can borrow their belief that you're on track and can achieve anything you want.

What are you doing today to get closer to your goal?

This leads to my last point of this chapter: I challenge you to help those around you and look for ways to encourage and hold others up. By encouraging others, you'll find that people will start encouraging you. It'll keep you focused on the positive energy you will need to reach your goal.

If you choose to do this through an app or other online community, great. If it's through writing in a journal, wonderful. If it's through sharing your goal with somebody close to you, perfect. Whatever you can do to keep your goal at the forefront of your mind is the right way because it is the way that works for you. Ask others about their goals, too, and cheer them on; create win-wins and embrace the infinite possibilities for all parties' success.

As a reminder: There is no growth or inspiration in goals that are easily attainable. Real growth and change will come from going after something you truly want and have no idea how to achieve.

One of the first steps toward positive change is to set a goal that will inspire you to do things that you would have never done before. Step out of your comfort zone into your learning zone. What can you do to get serious about reaching your goal? How can you step out of your comfort zone to get one step closer to that big dream? How can you encourage others to do this too?

What are you willing to do for your goal? Are you prepared to commit to doing the work to achieve it? What are you prepared to sacrifice? (I love this definition of sacrifice that my father often shared: "To sacrifice means to give up something of a lower nature for something of a higher nature." For example, you may choose to give up television time in the evenings for study or taking action toward your goal.)

These are the questions we must ask when going after big goals.

Remaining committed and overcoming inevitable obstacles takes work. When you hit the obstacles, bring your focus to what you can do right here, right now, at this very moment. All actions in the right direction count, no matter how seemingly small.

If you hit overwhelm, bring yourself back to this question: What can I do today to bring myself closer to my goal?

To create significant changes in your life, you need to act. Even if it is for only ten minutes at a time, it all adds up. And when you feel good about yourself, you end up being more, doing more, and having more. The Universe is willing to give you whatever you want. So stay in harmony with it by staying focused and taking small steps each day.

Life is too short to show up as anything other than your best. I also hope that by now you understand that you are capable of so much more than you have previously allowed yourself to imagine. Change comes from within, and that is the same for all of us. We are all works in progress. Let's celebrate this as we move forward together into the next chapter.

Key Points

- Set a big goal that is not easy to achieve but inspires you.
- Writing out your goal every day, especially first thing in the morning, sets you up for success.
- Share your goal only with people who will support you.
- Setting deadlines can be helpful for attaining your goal, but remember the date you choose is only a guess. Commit to it, but remain flexible.
- Find your cheerleader, and be someone else's.

3

WHAT CAN I DO TODAY?

This chapter is about becoming a leader. The leader in your own life and a leader for others. It's about becoming the person that others look up to and want to follow. And it's about making yourself and your goals a top priority.

My father was a great leader, but he was not a natural-born leader. It's a skill that he learned. His greatest leadership was in leading himself—and others followed. You see, as his awareness of how life works expanded, he became the star of his own movie.

I have discovered that this idea is the same for me. This is something that I have stepped into because I took control of my own life. Now it's your turn. You may not have realized it previously, but you're the casting director—you can make yourself the star. And this is not an ego play. You have the divine right to lead your own life. We all do.

We were put here on this earth to create and star in our own movies. Sadly, many of us go through most, if not all, of our lives, acting as an extra inside someone else's movie instead of stepping up to the plate as the leader we are meant to be.

By doing the work you have been doing here, you are becoming the star of your life, and by doing that, you will be leading yourself and others by example. You are evolving to higher levels of consciousness by increasing your awareness and understanding. You will teach others self-reliance through *your* self-reliance. And by becoming your own star, you're automatically giving others permission to become their own star as well—and that, my friend, is an amazing gift.

So what does this mean exactly—becoming the star of your own movie? You see, your life is your movie. And it starts with a question: What are you trading your life for?

You get to decide what you want. Many people get this backward, asking themselves, Am I worthy of this goal? The question we should be asking is, Is this goal worthy of me?

Have you answered that question yet? What do I really want? Can you clearly describe, with precision, what you really want?

Now think about this: You are writing the script for the movie of your life in every moment of the day. The words you speak, the thoughts you think, the emotions you feel—they're all part of your script. What is your theme? Drama or adventure? Comedy or suspense?

You see, most people don't realize they have the power to choose. So they let other people decide for them—this is what you will do for a living, this is where you will live, this is how you will help me build my dream and so on.

Starting today, decide that you will be making the decisions in your life. And make sure those decisions are lined up with where you want to go. Maybe you want a life with more passion, deeper relationships, a business you create. Whatever that is, you write it into your own script. You can still be a supporting player in the lives of others, but don't sacrifice your own starring role to do that. It's not necessary.

To get the most from this process, you've got to write a script that allows you to dream big while still believing that it's possible for you. Because if you don't believe it, you won't expect it, and that will keep your desire from moving toward you.

This really is about waking up and realizing that you are capable of so much more than you have allowed yourself to believe, that you've been playing small. And remember, a belief is just a thought that you keep thinking. So it's time to choose bigger, better, and more powerful thoughts about yourself and your life.

When I was twenty-six, I left my father's company for a while and began a career in real estate sales in Toronto. I was full of hope and excited to start this new chapter in my life. After I decided to go in this direction, my father sat me down to offer some advice. He told me, "Act as if you are the most successful real estate agent in the city of Toronto. It doesn't matter that you have never done this before. Meet with your client with the intention of providing value and service, listen closely to what they say, and act with confidence."

I followed that advice, and I was a pretty big success right from the start. It wasn't long before my name was at the top of the leaderboard in one of the top real estate brokerages in the country. I know this happened because I followed my father's advice.

My first clients had no idea how new I was. I went into every meeting embracing my father's words. I focused entirely on how I could provide service. I wasn't posturing, but rather I was committed to genuinely providing the best level of service to my clients that I or anyone else was capable of. I listened closely to what they were saying, and I also listened to what they weren't saying.

Nino, who was the broker for our office, had watched me closely. He asked me to put on a meeting with all the salespeople to explain what I was doing that had brought me so much success so quickly.

I remember thinking, boy, I'm kind of new at this. What is it that's created my results? When I got in front of the room to speak with the group, I candidly explained that my approach was straightforward. I told everyone, "Here's what I do. Each day, my entire focus is on what I can do right now to make a deal happen. Who can I call and connect with to get closer to securing a listing or making a sale? If I had free time, I would go out and knock on doors. I did whatever was necessary that day to make progress. When I was in front of a client, I treated that client as the most important person in the world and gave them my full attention."

Of course, I didn't close a deal every day, but with that focus, I achieved much more than most.

This way of conducting business came from my years of attending personal development seminars. My father would often talk about one story in particular from the stage that had a big impact on me. Let me tell it to you now.

He had just started to work with a large life insurance company in the 1970s. One day, when delivering a seminar to the company, he suggested to the audience of salespeople that they could break records for sales that year with ease if they listened to what he had to say. More specifically, he suggested to them that they had the ability to reach $5 million in sales each by the end of the year.

At the break, one of the insurance agents came up to my dad and suggested that my dad didn't know what he was talking about since he personally had never sold insurance. The agent said that no one has ever broken the kind of record he was talking about. Dad replied, "Well you could be the first!"

Well, that comment generated another response. This fellow exclaimed that the year was half over, so that would be an impossible feat. My father's next reply left him speechless.

Dad said, "Well, that's great, you can achieve that milestone in less time then."

When the meeting started back up, my father made one suggestion to the group. He said to make sure they are in front of a prospect every day before 9:00 a.m. and that they ask the prospect to purchase a specific amount of insurance. That's it! They didn't have to sell every prospect on that specific amount, they simply had to make the offer.

If they would do just that one thing, he said, records would be broken. He said it made no difference if the prospect bought or not, but they had to be face-to-face with someone and ask that question.

The man who had approached my father with skepticism and disbelief was named Don Sloven. Don went on to break the record that year, and continued to do so over the rest of his career. He was featured company-wide for his achievements.

What was the difference that moved the needle for Don? By doing just that one little thing every day, Don saw more prospects and made more sales. He took control of his day by focusing on what one thing he could do to make a deal happen. Because he did that, his sales skyrocketed along with his income. And I'd venture to say, he provided a greater level of sales to his company as well as to the people they served.

This is my challenge to you right now: What one thing can you do today that's going to get you one step closer to your goal? If you can stay focused on that every day, your life will never be the same. Dad used to say, "People frequently overestimate what they can do in a day, and underestimate what they can do in a year."

Often, we get caught in mundane routines and move mindlessly through our days—or we paralyze ourselves by thinking we must do something big and thereby do nothing at all. We may go out to lunch with a friend or get caught chatting with a colleague over coffee. Because of that, we don't accomplish nearly as much as we could.

If you will just focus on one thing you can do today that can get you one step closer to your goal, and you continue to do that every single day, it will build upon itself, just like the bricklayers laid brick after brick. Before long, you will be much further ahead of where you are right now.

Conquering Procrastination

One main obstacle when stepping out to create change is procrastination. Procrastination is almost like a disease, and a lot of people have it. If you tend to procrastinate, I have a very simple solution for you. That solution is to go back and read the previous chapter again.

You need to have a worthy goal. You need to have a reason to step out and act. You need to have something that's worth trading your life for! If you don't have a conscious, obvious, inspiring reason to jump out of bed every morning, you may fall into the procrastination trap. But if you have a goal that inspires you and excites you, a goal that gets you up in the morning with bright eyes, thinking—Okay, what can I do today?—you will eliminate procrastination from your life cold turkey.

When I'm inspired, I will do whatever it takes. I will contact whomever I need to contact and take whatever one step I need to take. The best way to eliminate procrastination is to be focused on something worthy.

The same is true with laziness. It's apathy—not wanting to do anything. I believe laziness is a habit. A habit that doesn't serve progress in your life. We can get past laziness when we're inspired. Lazy is easy but it's never the right answer. It eats away at your confidence and self-esteem and keeps you stuck right where you are in life with no vision of a more fulfilling future.

If that big thing is intimidating, or is not inspiring you enough to get moving and take daily action, what little thing can inspire you? What can you do today that's going to make you feel better about yourself today? If you start focusing on that, it may get you over the hump of doing nothing and out of the laziness trap.

The little thing can be something as simple as working out. As crazy as it may sound, sometimes my best workouts are when I don't feel like having a workout. I'm feeling lazy and drained. But I do it anyway, because I know it's the best choice. I know it is taking action. I do it, and afterward I think, Wow! I'm so glad

I pushed through that lazy feeling and did that workout. Sometimes using our willpower to push us will build an inner strength that is unmatched.

Overcoming Distraction

These days, everything feels urgent. You may feel motivated, even passionate, but then you get texts and emails that you feel you must respond to right away. Maybe they're from work; maybe they're from family. In any event, it's easy to arrive at the end of your day with nothing accomplished except putting out the fires of other people's stuff. You find yourself saying, "My day got away from me." Has this ever happened to you?

I admit I get distracted sometimes. The key is to organize your day so that you take focused action toward your key goal. That could mean turning your phone off and putting it in a drawer in a different room for a while. If you need to work on your computer, you can turn off notifications and close email. If that's what you need to do to get focused, that's what you need to do. I'm giving you permission. Get in the habit of giving yourself permission.

Proactively set yourself up for success by turning off your distractions, even if it's only for an hour at a time. Give yourself permission to delay responding to texts and emails. Most requests are not as urgent as you may think, or as others make them feel.

It's amazing what we can accomplish in one hour if we don't allow distractions to take over. Afterward, you can reward yourself and turn your phone back on and let the distractions fly.

Set yourself up for success by turning off distractions.

Creating habits that support you moving through your day with intention will work in your favor to minimize distractions that take you away from what's truly important to you. Focus on what you want to do right here, right now, and start taking steps. Multitasking is a myth that only serves to dilute efficiency and quality. When you narrow your focus to a chosen action, the next logical step will reveal itself, and you keep moving forward with intention.

If we zero in on that one next important goal, the distractions won't affect us the same way. When they do come in later, we've already accomplished our most important objective for the day, so it's no big deal. We've done what we needed to do that day, and it no longer inhibits success.

One major key is creating a block of time during which you're focused on one single thing. In this case, it's what you can do today that's going to get you one step closer to your goal. Ask yourself: How can I shut off the world and do something that's going to be productive and get me one step closer? Once I've done that, I'll open the world back up.

It's not going to be easy all the time, but it's a matter of discipline and practice. People may not understand, but don't concern yourself with that. The more you give yourself permission to do this and actually do it, the stronger and better you get at it. The rewards from acting this way will alter your life forever.

My father was a sterling example of these qualities. I watched the way he worked. He was like a scientist; he had it dialed in. He studied every single day. He would write in his journal every day. He rewrote his goal, and he looked for opportunities to take action. He would do whatever he could in a day to further his business and personal growth and, even more importantly, to help others. He was able to build his business while helping other people.

Often, he would help other people in their businesses without ever asking for anything in return. He would take his time to do whatever he could to help. Dad knew that the good he put out into the world would always return to him. He wouldn't know how, but he was solid in his belief and expectation that it would.

Dad had an incredible ability to focus. When it came to "busy work" he often taught the following: "Things often get done out of neglect." What he meant was that sometimes people bring things to you that they don't really need you for. Your inaction on those things, while you act on your bigger priorities, will cause them to take care of themselves.

That taught me a lot. It taught me the ability to give freely, help others when they needed help, and act from the heart. It also taught me to choose carefully what I put my attention into.

As I think back to the online memorial service we held for him, hundreds of thousands of people were online for this service. I don't believe any of us realized how well received he was in the world until that very moment. The comments emphasized how grateful they were for what my father gave—even to complete strangers. He was forever giving to people, always aiming to be of service. He would do whatever he could to help organizations and individuals, and he was very intentional with his actions. That's something that I learned from him: When you keep putting good out in the world, good must come back to you; that's a natural law.

The problem many of us have is that most of us believe that if we put out good to a given person, that person has got to give it back to us specifically. That's simply not the case. My father used to say this expectation is actually a model of "trading" and it's not truly giving.

We need to freely give. A person we give to may never have the means nor intention to give anything back in return. But when we give freely without any return expectations, the good will come back to us from somewhere. It might come back to us from a completely different source, and that's fine. If we can stay focused on living with a generous heart and mind no matter what, we'll attract better into our lives. It's really interesting. In fact, it's amazing.

The central point of this chapter is to do something to advance your goal every day. It doesn't necessarily have to take priority over everything; it's the dedication to doing something every day, in whatever way that is, big or small, that moves the needle. Stop waiting for that big thing. Ask yourself, What can I do today that's going to get me one step closer to my goal? If you keep doing that, it adds up over time. It's that simple.

By doing this, you become the star of your own movie and take control. And don't worry—you're still supporting others in even grander ways than before.

Key Points

- Focus on what you can do today.
- Inspiration can help you overcome procrastination.
- Organize your day to focus on your key goal.
- Eliminate distraction and carve out a block of time to focus on one single thing.

4

LIVE IN THE
PRESENT MOMENT

When I was a young boy, Dad always had hourglass-type sand timers around the house, and he usually took one onstage when he was speaking. He would use them as representations of life. The sand at the bottom represented our past, the sand at the top stood for our future, and the sand flowing through the neck was the present moment.

He would use this visual to illustrate that many people either dwell on the past—whether with regret or nostalgia—or fixate on the future with anxiety about what's coming next. Meanwhile, the present moment, where the sand is flowing right now, often gets overlooked. We have the tendency to let our minds wander to past events or future worries, missing out on the here and now. I know I've been guilty of this many times. How about you?

In these younger days, Dad would gently guide me back to the present moment. He'd ask what I was thinking and then remind me to return to the "now" with lessons like, "You can't change the time you got out of bed this morning." His point was clear: The past is unchangeable, but the present is where our choices matter.

By living in the present, we experience life more fully. It's about being mindfully engaged with our surroundings and paying attention to our thoughts. It's so easy to operate on autopilot, getting caught up in the daily trivia mentioned in a previous chapter. While this is a way many people live, I implore you to recognize that it's not really a life.

When we stay anchored in the present, we avoid the traps of regret from the past and anxiety about the future. We gain a sense of calm and control over our lives, connecting more deeply with our authentic selves and those around us.

Further reflecting on my childhood, I remember how Dad was always fully present when he was home. While many parents might be preoccupied with work or distractions like their phones, Dad was actively engaged. Whether we were playing catch in the backyard or having conversations, he was fully there, making me feel valued and important. This feeling of being valued and connected is what every person wants and certainly what every child deserves. These early lessons on presence have guided me throughout my life, and I am forever grateful.

When I was a teenager, we took a cross-country road trip from Toronto to Los Angeles with my brother and my sister in my dad's beloved Cadillac convertible. It was a great time, and Dad was always in the present moment with us. If somebody wanted to stop and do something, he'd say, "Let's do it." He wasn't worried about getting to LA on time. He knew we'd get there, and he wanted us to experience and enjoy the ride along the way.

I have always loved fishing. During that trip across the country, if I saw a river and wanted to fish, Dad stopped and let me go for it. I'd go fishing in the river for half an hour, and then we would carry on. The same was true when my brother and sister saw something they wanted to do. We saw the Petrified Forest. Also in Arizona, we checked out the Meteor Crater Landmark.

One evening, we saw a cheesy little motel that had a swimming pool in front of it, right by the road. We wanted to swim, so that's where we stopped for the night. Dad was showing us that our thoughts and desires mattered. He was simply a master at it.

It's easy to get so focused on a future ideal that we don't pay attention to or enjoy the present moment. I have good news for all of us. We can do both! We can enjoy this moment while taking actions that get us closer to our goal. This balance is key to feeling fulfilled and content.

Furthermore, the present is really the only time that actually exists. The past and the future do not exist at this moment. Things happened in the past, and other things will happen in the future, but the things that are happening right here, right now, are what's real.

**The present is the time
when you have control.**

Choosing to live in the present moment, especially when you are around others, will create good memories that you can look back on with a full heart. This could mean putting away your phone during a family dinner, fully engaging in a conversation with a friend, or appreciating the beauty of nature during a walk.

The Trap of Living in the Past and Future

We can easily see the problems with living in the past. For example, someone who was captain of the football team in high school feels his life has all been downhill from there. He keeps talking about the state championship and the big games, while right now in the present he's in his fifties. Peaking in life as a teenager is a sad way to live the rest of your life. There's value in being grateful for those experiences, but there's even more value in being grateful to be alive right now.

By contrast, people who are always living in the future often think that's good because it's about growth. Yet being excessively future-oriented presents problems as well. Yes, you need goals, but your success is what you experience along the way. Don't postpone your enjoyment of life into the future. Enjoy where you are right now, as you expect the next moment—and the next moment after that—to bring many more gifts.

If you only think about the future, you are likely experiencing some fear and uncertainty. So much time is wasted worrying about things that never happen. Dad often said, "Faith and fear both demand you to believe in something you cannot see."

Stop for a moment and think of something you recently spent time worrying about. Did it happen? I'm going to guess no. Yet energy was spent and wasted worrying about it—and it robbed you of the abundance and serenity of the present moment.

Those who live only in the future are wishing and dreaming, nothing more. They are not in the present or finding a way to take action and advance. When you bring yourself to your present moment, you're paying attention and you're doing something that will create a better future rather than just daydreaming about it. Remember, your thoughts, feelings, and actions in the now are actively creating your tomorrow.

We all know people who reached old age saying, with regret, "I coulda, I woulda, I shoulda." Decide right now that this will not be you. Instead, declare with calm, confident enthusiasm, "I am!"

The past holds incredible value as a teacher. It's a rich source of lessons from our mistakes and experiences. By reflecting on our past, we gain insights into what actions we should take in the present to move forward more effectively. We use these past experiences to guide our decisions, helping us understand what we truly want and what we want to avoid in our lives. As Joe Dispenza says, "The past without an emotional charge becomes wisdom in the present moment."

As I discussed in chapter 2, setting goals is about envisioning what we can achieve in the future. However, the key to living a fulfilling life lies in focusing on the present moment. It's in the here and now that we truly experience life. When we immerse ourselves in the present, we create a richer and more meaningful past to look back on. The more present we are now, the more vivid and rewarding our memories of the past will become.

Certainly, we all have moments to look back on and dreams to look forward to. The most effective approach is to stay anchored in the present moment when it comes to making meaningful improvements in any area of our lives—whether it's relationships, finances, business, or beyond. The question to ask yourself is this: What can I do right now?

Even though this mindset comes naturally to me now, I've faced my own struggles throughout my lifetime. During my divorce, I felt overwhelmed and vulnerable. It was an experience I hadn't anticipated or wanted, and, for a time, I withdrew and allowed that event to define me. Many people can relate to this feeling.

Then, a turning point came. Drawing from the lessons I've learned over the years, I realized I wasn't truly living. I was letting my past dictate my present and future. I was letting this painful experience define me. I suddenly understood that I didn't want that experience to continue shaping my life.

It was a moment of awakening that taught me the importance of reclaiming my focus on the present. Initially, I did this reframing little by little, and with time, I outgrew much of the pain.

My father had a simple but profound saying: "It is what it is." When I faced challenging times, I began to embrace this perspective. I would think, Well, it is what it is. What can I do right now to be a better version of myself? How can I take care of myself in this moment?

I focused on taking small, deliberate actions each day and tuned into my thoughts and self-talk. Whenever I found myself spiraling into negativity, I'd redirect my focus—whether by stepping outside, calling a friend, or listening to uplifting music. This practice of self-care made me feel valued and prioritized, and it can do the same for you. It often doesn't take much to shift from a low vibe to a higher vibe—the important point is that you do something and don't get perpetually caught up on the negative frequency for too long.

Of course, there were moments when I'd slip back into self-pity, but I quickly recognized it and gave myself a pep talk. That's the beauty of awareness. We may go to dark places at times, but we can bring ourselves right back into the light.

If you're reading this, you're on a journey of self-development just like I was. We all need to be aware when we're heading down a negative path and adjust course. Awareness is the key to transformation. And it gets easier and easier with practice.

By reading this book, you're increasing your awareness and considering new possibilities. You're creating new patterns, beliefs, and habits. Remember, it's all about choice—and awareness gives you the ability to choose. You get to decide which thoughts to entertain, which will shape your feelings and ultimately drive your actions and results. The best part? *You* are the one making those choices now, rather than old default patterns or personalities. Will you turn right or left? Each direction holds its own set of possibilities.

The Danger of Digital Devices

I've touched on the challenges digital devices present in today's world. They're everywhere, and while they bring us wonderful gifts and opportunities, they are double-edged swords since their constant distractions can be major obstacles to living fully in the present moment.

The sheer volume of notifications and alerts can create a background noise that we've become so accustomed to, we might not even notice the stress they are causing. But here's the key: You're in control and you set the boundaries. Don't follow the masses. Realize you're in charge.

In my own life, I keep tech simple. My phone is silent most of the time to minimize distractions. Sure,

I'll check it if I feel it vibrate, but I avoid letting it interrupt me with sounds or by carrying it around constantly. This approach aligns perfectly with a core message in this book: You are in control.

Affirm with me now: "I am in control." It's about setting the parameters for your life and focusing on what truly matters. And you get to define that for yourself.

As I reflect on people who truly embody the principles I discuss, one standout is someone I mentioned in the previous chapter—Nino, my broker from when I first ventured into real estate in my twenties. Nino wasn't just a broker; he became a close friend and a remarkable mentor. He had this incredible ability to be fully present.

When you were with Nino, you knew you had his complete attention. He wasn't scanning the room for someone else to talk to, and he wasn't distracted by the constant ringing of the phones in the office. He was always one hundred percent engaged.

Nino's kindness and generosity shone through in everything he did. He didn't just build a successful brokerage, he built a world-class organization through his genuine presence and attentiveness. People flocked to him because he made them feel valued and heard. Nino taught me a lot about the power of being truly present and how it can impact both personal and professional relationships.

We've all experienced those moments where you're having a conversation, and the other person's gaze is darting around the room, searching for their next interaction or preoccupied with what they're going to say. I'll bet if you think back, you've possibly caught yourself doing this too. It's never a pleasant experience. And again, with awareness, you can control whether you do this or not.

Looking at the flip side, it's truly impressive when you're with someone who is completely present with you, regardless of who else might walk in and no matter if their smartphone buzzes or beeps. You can feel their undivided attention and connection. That kind of presence speaks volumes about a person's character. It shows genuine respect and value for the interaction at hand. How will you choose to be with people moving forward?

Benefits of Living in the Present

Living in the present offers numerous benefits. A significant benefit is reduced anxiety about the future. By focusing on the present moment, you can set aside the past and the future and fully engage in what you're doing right now. This state of being allows you to be more fully alive so you can appreciate the richness of the present moment.

Everyone encounters challenges and setbacks, but when you intentionally focus on the moment you are in, those past difficulties don't overshadow your thoughts, even if the difficulty presented itself just ten minutes ago. When you are present, the difficulties don't occupy your mental space. By focusing on the here and now, you free yourself from the grip of past grievances and can truly be the best version of yourself. Enjoy the present moment for all it has to offer, and you'll find yourself living more vibrantly and authentically.

**You can be the best version
of you right here and now.**

Practical Tips for Staying Present

To enhance your ability to stay present, try these practices:

- **Engage fully with others.** When interacting with someone, make eye contact and listen. It's difficult to stay present if your attention is elsewhere, and others will notice when you're fully engaged because it will make them feel important.

- **Try focus exercises.** My father taught me to focus on the flame of a candle. When your mind drifts, gently bring it back to the flame. This simple practice strengthens your ability to stay present with what is in front of you. Plus, the flame is like a living, breathing object that is fascinating to look at when you're tuned in to its beauty.

- **Take short breaks.** If you find yourself losing focus in the present moment or feeling fatigued, take a fifteen-minute meditation break and let your mind go. Deep breathing and sensory awareness can rejuvenate you and improve productivity.

- **Conduct regular awareness checks.** Periodically ask yourself if you're fully present. Are you truly engaged with your surroundings and the people around you? If not, gently redirect your focus back to the present moment. This is especially important for those of us living and working in the digital age with VR and AI becoming more and more prevalent.

By incorporating these practices, you can enhance your ability to live in the present, reduce stress, and improve your overall quality of life. Remember, 99 percent of life is showing up, and you can't show up if you're lost in the past or preoccupied with the future. Your body may be there, but your mind and soul are not home.

Short breaks are powerful tools to help you refocus and stay in the present moment.

The most important practice in this regard is the simplest. Recognize if you're present and think about this often. When you're with somebody, are you really with them? Are you engaged with them, or are you somewhere else mentally? If you're with your kids, are you really with your kids? Do they feel that you're with them? If you're with your spouse, are you really with your spouse? If you're by yourself out in the woods, are you enjoying the woods?

Mentally, take note of where your thoughts are. When you realize your mind has wandered, gently bring it back to the present moment. Don't beat yourself up—instead, congratulate yourself on your awareness and recommit to doing better.

Key Points

- Living in the present helps you avoid regrets about the past and anxieties about the future.
- Being present allows you to truly live your life.
- Practice concentration to boost your ability to stay present.
- Short relaxation breaks can reinvigorate your focus and productivity.
- Regularly check your engagement with the present moment and gently refocus when needed.

5

LIFE SCRIPTS AND AFFIRMATIONS

In this chapter, we'll delve into two powerful tools: life scripts and affirmations. These concepts technically are separate and unique from each other, but they work together beautifully to transform your life.

Affirmations

As the name suggests, affirmations are affirming. They are simple, positive statements from ourselves to ourselves that can help shift our mind in ways that improve our overall well-being.

Start by crafting a positive statement that resonates deeply with you. Then, read it aloud every day until it becomes a part of who you are; this means you can feel the truth of it in your body—you believe it. For example, an affirmation related to your health could be, "I am perfectly healthy, and I appreciate that I get to live my life in a wonderful body."

An affirmation is a powerful practice for developing better habits and building confidence and self-image. When you engage your affirmation with positive emotions and behaviors, you will take different actions that create better results. This will cause you to feel differently—likely more positive toward yourself. This shift enables you to be stronger and better at anything you decide to do. Remember, the person you need to love first is yourself.

Here are two key points when creating affirmations: They should be positive and stated in the present tense. As you repeat them daily, you'll notice a shift in how you perceive yourself and your potential. For an added layer of impact, consider inspirational author Louise Hay's mirror work technique. She has suggested you read your affirmations to yourself in the mirror. It might initially feel awkward—I know it did for me!—but it's a meaningful way to connect deeply with your inner self.

Give it a try; you've got nothing to lose. Affirmations are invaluable tools that anyone can benefit from.

Life Scripts
Creating a life script is a technique introduced to me by my friend Peggy McColl. She would write out her ideal

life a year into the future, framing it as if it already happened and writing it like a movie script. Peggy would create a handwritten script, filled with positive, congratulatory language and then record it in her own voice.

She'd start the recording with, "This is my power life script. Everything is coming to be. I am so happy and grateful now that—" And she listened to it daily. The results she achieved with this approach were extraordinary to witness.

Like positive affirmations, this tool can trigger change because you're reprogramming your subconscious mind with these new, positive ideas. By listening to your ideal life on repeat in this way over many days, weeks, and months, you're beginning to feel what it would be like to have achieved those things, because you're speaking it as if it's already happened. It allows you to get comfortable with what may have previously made you uncomfortable. And it's compatible with Earl Nightingale's wisdom that "we become what we think about most of the time."

Initially, I tried Peggy's method, but listening to my own voice didn't resonate with me. My wife, Cory, has a beautiful voice that I love listening to, so I had her record my life script for me. Hearing her warm, encouraging words felt like a heartfelt embrace, deeply connecting me with my vision in both my subconscious and my heart. This technique became one of the most powerful tools I've ever used.

The more I listened to my life script, the more real it became, and I found myself taking new actions and seeing new opportunities. Even though I've achieved everything in that script today, I still listen to it occasionally. It's a reminder of how far I've come and how I got there. In fact, it's about time that I create a new one for my next chapter of life.

What sounded far-fetched at the start is now my reality. Using this technique opened me up for the good that I desired. It made me feel than I owned it, that I deserved it, and that I could do it. Eventually, I started doing the things that were required to get there, and before I knew it, I was living that life script in full living-color—in the real world.

I challenge you to embrace this technique. Write out your life as if it's a year from now. Describe where you are, what you're doing, and how you're feeling. For instance, you could write, "I am living in a beautiful house in the countryside, driving a sleek car, feeling healthy and vibrant, surrounded by loving family and friends, treating them with respect and kindness, and being treated the same way."

Take your time and write it all out. Be as specific as you can with your current level of desires and awareness, but don't worry about making it perfect. Record it yourself or have a loved one read it aloud and record it for you. Listen to the script daily—it will transform your mindset and approach to life.

It may sound too good to be true, but if you're skeptical, remember, what have you got to lose? I've tested this out myself and know it works. Everything I'm sharing with you throughout this book has stood the test of time, and not just for me, but for many.

Understanding the Technique

Some might wonder if scripting your life is realistic. I believe it aligns with the law of attraction: What you focus on, you attract. Your thoughts, focus, and actions determine what you bring into your life. By focusing on your desires, you start to align with them. That enables you to take positive action toward that vision with positive reinforcement.

As you continue, you might find that your goals evolve. That's perfectly fine. Update your script as needed to reflect your current desires. For example, if you initially wrote about a career goal of becoming a teacher and you later decide this is not what you truly desire, you can update your script to reflect your new aspirations as a programmer. The key is to listen daily and let it guide your actions. Your belief in what is possible for you will evolve to higher levels as you study and practice the steps laid out here.

My father always said, "Once you set a goal and achieve it, you realize you were aiming lower than you could have gone with an equal amount of effort." His point was that we're always evolving, and our potential is unlimited. The only limits are the ones we impose upon ourselves. As we progress forward, our self-image and self-belief improves, and we realize we can do even more.

Affirmations and life scripts are powerful tools for aligning your thoughts with your goals and nurturing a positive mindset. They work hand in hand to help you reshape your self-image. By using these techniques, you'll start to see yourself in a new light, making it easier to embrace the good things you want in your life. They'll also sharpen your focus on your goals and steer you in the direction you want to go. While affirmations and life scripts won't magically manifest your desires on their own, they will guide you toward action in the direction of your desires. It is all about mindset.

As mentioned in the introduction, my father appeared in *The Secret*, which focused on the law of attraction—essentially, what you think about, you bring about. But he pointed out something crucial that the movie didn't cover in detail: You must take action toward your dreams and goals.

Affirmations and life scripts are fantastic tools for aligning your thoughts and energies with what you want to attract. They help you stay focused on your desires and envision the life you want. However, they're not a substitute for action. The real power comes from stepping out and taking concrete steps each day toward your goals. These tools set the stage for you to act by conditioning your mind to see and seize the possibilities.

**The law of attraction:
What you think about, you bring about.**

Let's revisit one of the key themes we've covered: staying present and focusing on the one thing you can do today. Affirmations and life scripts are your tools for honing that focus and steering you toward goal-aligned action. When you act on these tools, you're actively moving toward your goals and making them a reality.

Think of life scripts and affirmations like the steering wheel of a car. They help keep your mind aligned with your goals and steer you in the right direction. Without them, it's like driving without a clear sense of direction—your focus can drift, and you may find yourself going off course. Having the wheel is just part of the equation; you still need to step on the gas to move forward.

I remember when I first got my motorcycle license in my twenties. During the course, the instructor said, "The motorcycle will go wherever you're looking. If you're staring at the ditch, you will end up in the ditch. Always look where you want to go." This advice proved to be spot-on. When riding, if my gaze wandered, so did the bike. It's exactly the same in life—where you direct your focus, that's where you'll head.

Make sure you're looking where you want to go.

These tools are like a steering wheel for your life—they keep you focused on where you want to go. Without them, you risk letting external influences, like media or negative people, steer you off course and toward outcomes you don't desire.

In today's world, you have a choice: You can take control and craft your own life script, or you can let others dictate it for you.

When setting your goals, aim high. Choose something that challenges you and pushes you beyond your comfort zone. Your goal should spark a fire within, motivating you to reach for what seems just beyond your grasp.

For me, my initial life script was a significant stretch. However, I was raised with the belief that dreaming big and pursuing lofty goals was the way to go. I learned early on that nothing is out of reach. If you can envision your future and truly believe in it, you can achieve it. That's the mindset I grew up with, and it's one that has guided me throughout my life.

Not everyone starts with grand visions, and that's perfectly okay. If a big goal feels out of reach, begin with something smaller and more manageable.

For instance, you could focus on building deeper connections in your life. Set a goal to spend just fifteen minutes a day reaching out to someone—make a phone call, write a letter, or send an email message. Create an affirmation such as, "I am so happy and grateful to be deeply connecting with the people in my life every day." Write a life script that reflects similar actions and experiences.

Do this consistently for thirty days. At the end of that period, reflect on how these daily interactions have impacted your relationships and your own growth.

This practice of setting and pursuing a goal is the foundation for bigger aspirations. As you use the tools in this book, you'll gradually set more ambitious goals, ones that might seem beyond your current reach. You'll find excitement in envisioning them, and you'll develop daily habits that bring you closer to achieving them. Before you know it, they'll start to feel smaller, and your belief in their achievement will skyrocket.

A goal should challenge you and encourage growth, pushing you beyond your comfort zone. It doesn't need to be outlandish, but it should be a step beyond what feels safe. Remember, goals are meant to transform who you are through what you experience along the way to your goal. They are meant to enhance your circumstances.

Set a goal that makes you think, "Even if I don't yet know how to achieve this goal, this is a vision of a truly rewarding life. This is where I want to focus my energy."

When crafting your life script, think of it as a personal letter of congratulations to yourself. Outline the achievements you're aiming for while you paint a vivid picture of your future success: "I'm so proud of you for reaching this milestone, living in this incredible home, and growing your business to this level." Make your script heartfelt and expressive. No script is too long or too short. Mine tend to be up to about two minutes in length, while Peggy's might be thirty. It's just whatever works and feels good to you.

When you record it, let the tone of your voice convey genuine pride and enthusiasm. Play with it and have fun. Listen to your life script daily—not just for a month, but as a continual practice. The power of repetition will anchor these aspirations deeply within you. Make it a source of inspiration you look forward to, not just another task.

When it comes to listening to your recording, consistency is crucial. Peggy, for example, immersed herself in her recording multiple times a day, demonstrating remarkable dedication. You might not need to go that far, but regular listening is essential to truly embed your future vision into your mind. Listening at least twice per day—once in the morning and once before bed is advisable.

I didn't quite go to Peggy's level of intensity, but I made it a habit to listen to my recording every morning upon waking. I used it almost like a meditation—earbuds in, eyes closed, absorbing the message. The key is to really feel it. I internalized what I was hearing, visualizing my future as if it were already happening. This practice allowed me to alter my paradigms and reshape how I viewed life and expand what I believed was possible. It's a powerful way to change your mindset and embrace the reality you're working toward.

I am now living the life that I imagined and recorded just a few short years ago. I know this technique was a big part of helping me get there. Trust me when I say I had some big things in my life script, especially relative to my present reality back then. And that was the key to my success.

Life scripts and affirmations are tools for changing your thinking—for remapping your mind and changing your perspective to see your life and the direction of your life as hopeful and positive. It's a way to create positive paradigms, a positive self-image, and a positive way of being. This is a way to program your mind for a better outcome.

We're getting programmed every day through family, friends, television, social media, and any number of other sources—usually without even realizing it. Why not take conscious control of how your mind is being programmed by using affirmations and life scripts?

See the following for some example affirmations that you can use on their own or embed into your life script.

Key Points

- Embrace the transformative power of positive affirmations. Craft statements that resonate with you and read them daily until they become a fundamental part of who you are. This practice will spark hope and inspiration within you and will help you activate the laws of attraction and vibration frequently throughout your day.
- Ensure your affirmations are (1) positive and (2) phrased in the present tense. This alignment is vital for creating a powerful impact.
- In your life script, write a vivid narrative of your ideal future, detailing how you want your life to unfold a year from now. Use present-tense

language as if you are already living this ideal life. This technique helps anchor your vision in reality.

- Record your life script and listen to it at least once a day. This repetition will help you internalize your vision and keep it at the forefront of your mind.
- The law of attraction is a potent force: What you focus on and feel with emotion, you attract. Therefore, ensure your affirmations and life script are centered on your desired outcomes and include vivid emotional experiences. This focus is essential for manifesting what you truly want.

Sample Affirmations

Here are the affirmations I used in the 1980s when I was a real estate agent. I spoke these out loud every day:

- I am a total success. Things go my way in life. All my efforts bring rich rewards.
- I set high goals for myself, which I am able to attain. I am a warm and friendly person, and people are naturally drawn to me. People seek me out to do business with me.
- I am totally relaxed and confident in making presentations.

- I feel positive at all times, and people respond to me in a positive way. I powerfully attract more and more customers to my business.
- It is becoming easier and easier for me to realize my sales goals. My positive, enthusiastic attitude is infectious.
- People want to buy from me. My customers recommend me to others, and the number of my customers is increasing daily.
- My sales are increasing dramatically. My income level is rising higher and higher.
- I am a success at everything I do. Everything goes my way and works out positively for me.
- I have a magnetic personality and attract people to my business. More and more money is coming to me.
- All my efforts are productive. I believe in myself completely. I am attaining my sales goals. Nothing can deter me from my goals.
- My income level is increasing dramatically. I have total confidence and know I am a winner in life.
- Money comes to me easily.
- It is okay to make more money than Dad.
- I deserve riches. Success is mine. Prosperity is mine.

6

EXERCISE

Exercise is a very important part of life. In fact, I believe it is essential for a healthy body, mind, and soul.

Moving doesn't just keep our body in great shape—it keeps our brain fit and well too. It fosters the physical ability for energy to flow to and through us, from head to heart to toe.

We were designed to move; your body is your vessel for this life. A bonus is that when we intentionally move throughout the day and exercise, we feel better about ourselves. We are creating more blood flow and setting ourselves up to win. It's triggering all kinds of positive bonuses from a hormonal and physiological perspective. And when we feel better about ourselves, we're more effective in all areas of our lives.

When my father was in his seventies, he hired a personal trainer. Even at that age, he understood the crucial importance of maintaining a healthy body. His goal was to keep his stamina high so he could continue delivering his material from the stage right up until his last breath.

One of the many traits I admired about my dad was his passion. He became incredibly passionate about his personal trainer and the work they were doing together. His enthusiasm was contagious, and, soon enough, he had the entire family working with his coach. For me, this meant driving quite a distance four days a week to join these workout sessions. The workouts were intense, and they focused on building muscle and bulking up.

As good as I was feeling, I eventually realized that this approach didn't align with my personal goals and vision. So I stepped back from his workout routine and started doing exercises that suited my own objectives.

My dad appreciated that the trainer's approach mirrored his teachings on making any paradigm shift. The trainer emphasized raising awareness through information, action, repetition, and, ultimately, results.

For me, the quality of my life is central to every goal I set. Staying active in ways that keep me healthy and having fun at the same time nourish my soul and make everything else I do easier.

Find a type of exercise that meets your objectives.

I realize we all have different body types, body shapes, physical abilities, and different versions of health and what exercise is. I'm not saying you need to be Mr. or Ms. Universe by any stretch of the imagination. All the same, I do believe that with some simple exercise every day, your body will feel better, your brain will be a little clearer, and you will approach life with more energy.

Exercise gets us into a better, more energized state. If you're looking to create great things in your life, exercise is an important component because it gets you fit and enables you to do whatever's required. You feel better about yourself, so naturally you're going to be more effective.

This doesn't mean you need to spend multiple hours in the gym seven days a week. Instead, incorporate movement into your day. Park farther from the store, take the stairs, and add squats to household chores. Don't underestimate a simple walk, especially after dinner. Walking improves attention and memory and slows cognitive decline while reducing anxiety and stress. It also protects against heart disease, high blood pressure, and type 2 diabetes. Exercise can improve sleep and enhance mood. The key is to take action and find your self-discipline.

Personally, I love the Peloton bicycle. I like joining in the live classes where I'm competing against a few thousand other riders. It brings me joy. At the time of this writing, I'm sixty-two, and I love it when I can outperform the thirty-somethings on the Peloton bike. I'm a little competitive in the physical department, so it's important and fun for me. Using my competitive nature causes me to work harder and get better results. When I exercise, I feel better, and my day is better.

I also love to go for hikes into the woods, see and smell the trees, and be in nature. Even getting up for a walk makes you feel better and fresher. To affirm an earlier point, getting out in nature puts you in the present moment and clears your head so you can get back to your most important and immediate tasks. Being in nature changes your vibration, and when you go out and leave your devices behind, you will free your mind to benefit from that vibration—ideas will come to you. You will solve problems you've been grappling with by changing your scenery and giving yourself space to breathe. It's even more powerful if you couple being in nature with some sort of exercise activity.

I admit that my exercise routines have been off and on throughout my life. When I was younger, I exercised a lot. However, in middle age, there were times when I would fall off the wagon. I wouldn't exercise much. I'd gain weight, feel tired and frustrated, and reach a point where I'd look in the mirror and say, "Brian, what are you doing?" I realized I needed to start exercising again for my mental and physical well-being.

Of course, it's hard to get back into exercising once the momentum has stalled, but you know that when you take up a regimen again, over time your body will get back into shape, and you'll feel better—you can get right back into some beautiful momentum. It worked for me and also has for countless others.

Now, I've formed the habit of exercising, and it's become a part of who I am. It's not that I must; it's that I want to. And when we want to do something, it no longer feels like an obligation. I don't have to exercise—I get to exercise!

In general, it's best to start small. The easiest way to fall out of an exercise routine is to try to do too much at once. It's like the advice in this book: If you try to tackle all twelve chapters at once, you're probably not going to do any of them. You'll quickly fall off. Once again, stop waiting for that big thing.

Exercise is the same way. You don't want to start as if you're aiming for the Olympics. Instead, develop a habit of increasing daily movement and adding some form of exercise. If it's a twenty-minute walk, go for a twenty-minute walk. Those twenty minutes will pass whether you're sitting on the couch or out walking, and you'll feel better if you choose to walk. Then let the activity grow from there. Maybe next time, you walk for twenty-five minutes. Just build on it gradually.

Creating change is very rarely easy; it takes discipline, effort, and mental fortitude. But if you stay focused on the outcome, you'll be in better shape and have a clearer mind, which will make you more effective in your professional and personal life.

Do What You Enjoy

With so many fitness options available today—CrossFit, interval training, marathon running, cycling, yoga—

choosing one can be overwhelming. I'm not an expert, but I'd suggest doing what feels right for you and brings you joy. Do what makes you happy. Personally, I enjoy cycling and walking in the woods so that is what I do. When you do activities you enjoy, the odds of your sticking with it have increased dramatically.

We can listen to all the noise that surrounds us online and on television, but it all comes down to the same message: If you don't enjoy exercise, you're not going to do it for long. You might do it for a week or a couple of weeks, but if you're not enjoying it, you're not going to stick with it. In short, do some form of movement, but do the form that resonates with you. If you enjoy it even a little, you'll stick with it longer, and you'll see positive results.

Once you've developed an exercise routine, the time you devote to it may vary. It may be twenty minutes or a half hour. For myself, it would be an hour to an hour and a half every day. Sometimes, it might be a little bit more, and sometimes it might be a little bit less, but that's what works for me.

Naturally, we all have various tasks to attend to each day. You can't spend the entire day exercising, but I firmly believe it's essential to do enough to improve your well-being and enhance your physical condition. The benefits are substantial. You'll gain a significant boost in energy, and you can channel that energy into other productive actions.

Reflecting on a few years back, I remember a time when regular exercise wasn't part of my routine. I needed a nap almost daily and felt constantly drained in the middle of the day. However, since I committed to exercising properly again, I've never had to nap and no longer experience that midday fatigue. I feel better overall and perform more effectively at work. Including movement and exercise in my daily schedule has always been the right choice. I've never regretted it.

For those of us in our sixties, cardiovascular exercise holds undeniable value. Equally important is strength training. Engaging in strength training can significantly enhance your lifespan and overall health. It's crucial for longevity, balance, mental sharpness, and physical strength. Most importantly, it supports our ability to live independently.

Many studies are out there, and they can be skewed in all kinds of different ways. Even so, I think it comes down to this: A person in motion will stay in motion and will accomplish more. A person who is not in motion becomes stagnant. And the old adage is true—use it or lose it. This includes our muscles. Again, you get to choose. No one else can do this for you.

A person in motion will stay in motion and will accomplish more.

The key is to keep moving. Enjoy the process. You'll feel better about yourself. When you're exercising, your self-image will improve, and you will become more effective in accomplishing your goals.

Nutrition

When it comes to overall health, nutrition goes hand in hand with exercise. Personally, I'm very mindful of what I eat and how I eat. I avoid processed foods almost entirely. I live by the rule, "Eat real food, not too much, mostly plants." My wife, Cory, often reminds me, "Eat to live, don't live to eat."

When I shop for groceries, I stick to the outer edges of the store. That's where you'll find fresh produce and fresh meats. The middle aisles are filled with processed foods, which I avoid. I steer clear of boxed items and try to avoid eating large portions, opting instead for just enough to satisfy my hunger comfortably.

There's a vast amount of information out there about exercise and nutrition, and it can be overwhelming. You might feel pressured to follow every new trend or piece of advice. But I believe it's simple: Stay active doing something you enjoy. Eat wholesome, whole food that you enjoy. Work to maintain a positive mindset. And don't eat based on your emotions—whether they're particularly high or low on any given day.

As you settle into your routine, you might become interested in more advanced forms of exercise or specific dietary plans. That's fine, but don't let the flood of information distract and overwhelm you in the beginning—keep it simple. Just focus on doing something active and enjoyable. The important point is to start. The rest can come later as you get more comfortable and confident in your routine.

Key Points

- Fitness enhances your ability to reach your life goals.
- Start small with your exercise program.
- Do the type of exercise that you enjoy.
- Eat the healthy foods that you like best and separate your emotional rhythms from your food consumption.

7

DO WHAT BRINGS YOU JOY

The essence of this chapter is a truth we all understand but often fail to incorporate into our daily lives: Pursuing what brings us joy is fundamental to a fulfilling life.

One often overlooked benefit of engaging in joyful activities is that they make you a more vibrant and engaging individual. When you immerse yourself in what brings you happiness, you enrich your life and gain experiences worth sharing with others. While doing what brings you joy may initially sound selfish or self-serving, it's anything but, because when you're well, you help others be well.

This pursuit can provide peace of mind, even amid life's chaos. No matter the challenges in your business or personal life, engaging in joyful activities can alleviate anxiety and reinforce your sense of purpose, reminding you of who you are and why you're here. Joyfulness is a deep state of being that results in feelings of inner peace and contentment.

A good friend of mine has crafted a personal mission statement from which he lives that I absolutely love. It says, "My purpose in life is to enjoy the rest of my life and help others enjoy theirs!" What a great intention for living.

I have a deep passion for fishing and spending time on the water. Just before my father passed away, he said to me, "Brian, make sure you get out and fish. Enjoy the water. Make it a priority to do things that bring you joy because that's what life is truly about. Achieving great things and helping others is important, but don't forget to stop and smell the flowers. That's when you're truly living."

I took his advice to heart. For me, it's usually being out on the water, whether in a kayak or a boat, or sometimes just relaxing in the hot tub. Incorporating these joyful activities into my day not only fills me with happiness but also makes me more productive and provides a sense of calm.

Deep down, we all know which activities fill our soul. Let this chapter serve as a reminder to prioritize joy in your life. Without it, you risk getting bogged down by the minutiae of daily living. By carving out time each day for something that makes your heart sing, you can achieve better balance and, in my belief, greater happiness. Identify what creates moments of awe in your life and touches the deepest part of your soul. Incorporating these joyful activities will add a profound richness to your life and enhance your overall well-being and fulfillment.

Although it may seem obvious that we need to make time for joy in our lives, many people grapple with guilt about doing so. They think, "I need to struggle and strive toward my goals first, and only then can I afford to relax and enjoy my life. Until then, focusing on anything but goals can feel like laziness."

Let me be clear: Pursuing goals doesn't mean you must forgo joy along the way. You can be diligent about your goals while also making time to laugh, connect, exhale, and have fun.

Embracing a life that includes these activities will provide more stability and help you navigate challenges more effectively. There will always be people who feel they must complete all their tasks and achieve all their goals before enjoying life. However, you could spend your entire life being responsible and never experience joy if you don't make room for it. Prioritizing joy alongside your ambitions ensures a smoother road to success in all areas of your life. And remember, regardless of how many years you end up being on this planet, life, in the grand scheme of things, is incredibly short.

Being responsible doesn't mean sacrificing what makes life important and meaningful. Reaching goals and success will feel empty if we have lost the ability to connect with others and enjoy life.

People who continually push themselves hard are often driven by deeper, unresolved issues. A relentless, guilt-driven drive that doesn't allow for joyful activities is a recipe for burnout. It's a form of self-punishment rooted in past failures or conditioning that leaves a person feeling perpetually inadequate. Is this you? Then pay special attention to this chapter, and read it daily for the next thirty days.

The irony is that pausing to engage in what brings joy is the antidote to this destructive mindset. It's crucial to release that attitude and let go of past regrets. We can't change what's happened; we can only improve who we are today. Part of that improvement involves loving ourselves enough to seek out what makes us smile and intentionally engage in activities that bring us joy.

Discovering and learning to embrace what gives life deeper meaning can be a transformative experience. It can make you a better version of yourself, enhancing your roles as a spouse, parent, and businessperson. When you allow yourself to experience the lighter side of life, you become more engaged, more grounded, and more connected to the world around you.

Learning to live fully in the present moment comes from doing what you love. It's less about achieving a specific outcome and more about being present and connected to what is real. The concept of experiencing rather than merely doing can be lost on many people. Life is not about muscling through; it's about fully participating and immersing yourself in each moment. Embrace the richness of the present and savor the experiences that bring you true satisfaction.

When I was younger, riding motorcycles brought me immense pleasure, especially during tough times. Riding provided a sense of freedom and helped me escape my worries. Today, being on the water gives me that same sense. Both activities broaden my perspective and help me shift focus from my problems to the sensory experiences of joy.

Balance is essential for a fulfilling and productive life. Constantly pushing forward without pause can be exhausting and unsustainable. However, intentionally incorporating regular breaks into our routine can enhance efficiency and productivity across all areas of our life. By allowing ourselves moments to rest and recharge, we maintain higher levels of focus and energy, ultimately improving our overall performance. These breaks provide an opportunity to reflect, rejuvenate, and return to our tasks with renewed vigor and clarity. Remember, true productivity comes from a harmonious blend of hard work and intentional downtime.

Some individuals, unfortunately, find a twisted sense of satisfaction in others' misfortunes, but this ultimately harms their own soul. True joy arises from inner peace and a heart filled with love. When your heart is full of love, you cannot find pleasure in others' troubles.

In today's turbulent world, protecting your inner peace is essential. Avoid letting negativity seep into your soul. Actively seek the good in life, and it will find you. By taking control of your own journey, being the star of your own movie, you empower yourself to maintain your inner peace and happiness—which, fortunately, is contagious and also beneficial to others. Embrace positivity and love, and let them guide you toward a more fulfilling and joyful existence.

Bright Examples of Joy

One vivid example of a joyful spirit is my neighbor Ann. She embodies joyful living in everything she does. As a hospice and palliative care nurse, Ann knows the value of joy deeply. She's often out in a kayak or traveling, living for experiences rather than material possessions. Her constant smile and enthusiasm for life, even at social gatherings, is infectious. She lives from a place of joy, and being around her is uplifting.

A few years back, my wife and I embarked on a journey to Africa. We joined a group dedicated to raising funds for schools in the Maasai Mara region of Kenya.

When we visited these schools, we saw children with bare feet, their families unable to afford shoes. Most lived in modest huts with dirt floors and no running water, having to walk a mile to fetch water from a river. By our standards, their conditions seemed quite harsh. Yet, despite their lack of material wealth, their smiles were the broadest I've ever encountered. They embodied the essence of living in the moment and cherishing what they had. Their joy wasn't tied to possessions but to their appreciation of life itself. While many in North America might view such poverty as a bleak existence, these children were dancing, laughing, and radiating happiness.

Witnessing this was profoundly moving for me. It became a turning point in my understanding of joy. I realized that true joy isn't about material abundance—it's an inside job, a state of mind. It's about finding happiness and fulfillment from within. I've seen people with plenty of money who lack joy, connection, and laughter. Now, if you are short on money, that might sound appealing. But not having connection, laughter, and happiness is a very lonely and sad way to live. It's a stark reminder that joy comes from within and isn't dependent on external circumstances.

The Key

The key is straightforward: Discover what brings you joy. Is it a bicycle ride? A day on the water in a kayak? A few frames at the bowling lanes? Perhaps it's calling a loved one, relaxing on your front porch, or baking cookies for a neighbor.

Identify what resonates with you and make time to engage in that activity, even if it's just one game of bowling or a brief walk in the park. Joy manifests in many forms. What truly fills your heart? What brings you peace? Seek that answer and embrace it fully. Let these activities be part of your daily life.

I refer to this process as centering. It's about grounding yourself in positive experiences and feeling alive and connected. It revitalizes your spirit and fosters a deep sense of connection. You don't need to wait to achieve your goals to experience joy. It's a choice you can make now. It's an emotion available for you to feel immediately.

Whatever activity brings you joy, make it a priority. Stop making excuses for why you can't engage in some pursuit. We can come up with reasons to avoid almost anything. Instead, choose to embrace what fills your spirit as if it were a prescription from the doctor. You'll find that activity profoundly elevates your life. And speaking of prescriptions, we now have science that shows how being in states of joy and gratitude can release natural chemicals inside our bodies that elevate our health and can even heal chronic health conditions.

Balancing your pursuit of goals with moments of joy will make you more creative and productive in all other areas of your life. Embracing this way of being, alongside your ambitions, ensures a more balanced, fulfilling life journey. Do this with intention and watch as your life transforms in remarkable ways.

Key Points

- You don't have to achieve your big goal to start experiencing happiness. Activities that bring you joy are available right now.
- True contentment isn't tied to material abundance. You can feel fulfilled regardless of how much or how little you have.
- Prioritize activities that genuinely bring you joy. Make time for them and let them enrich your life.

8

THE FIVE THINGS LIST

The five things list is a tool for significantly enhancing your productivity. It will enable you to accomplish more in less time and free you up for joyful activities, such as spending quality time with family, pursuing a hobby, or engaging in self-care.

My father shared a story about the first time he met inspirational speaker Earl Nightingale. After sitting down across from each other at a lunch table, he asked Earl how he managed his time and became so effective.

Even decades after asking this question, Dad said he could still hear the sound of Earl's fork dropping and hitting his plate. Earl looked at him and said, "We don't manage time. Time can't be managed. We just have what there is. You know, everybody gets the same amount of time. What we manage are activities."

Earl said that each night he would write out six things he would accomplish the next day. When Earl woke, he used that list as a compass, and he would start at number one and focus on that one task until it was done, and then and only then go to number two. He was managing his activities, not time. This means focusing on the tasks at hand, prioritizing them, and completing them one by one, which he found allowed him to accomplish far more than bouncing around from item to item.

We don't manage time.
We manage our activities.

Understanding this concept puts us in the driver's seat, giving us the power to direct our day and our productivity, releasing the false idea that we can manage time, which Earl pointed out is a pointless and impossible goal.

The idea of focusing on managing activities rather than time really resonated with me. I grew up absorbing Earl Nightingale's insights, and I first met him when I was about nine or ten years old. His approach made complete sense to me. I decided to adopt Earl's method and created my own daily list of goal-oriented tasks, inspired by my favorite number, fifty-five. However, I realized that fifty-five tasks might be a bit much, so I settled on five. It's a perfect balance—manageable and effective.

The List of Five Process

Here's how the process works: Each night, write down five goal-achieving activities you want to achieve the next day. These should be goal-oriented activities that advance your productivity, income, or personal growth.

Now, keep in mind, these steps don't have to be outrageous, but they do need to keep you on track. For example, it could include making a phone call to someone you want to learn something from. What you don't want on that list are things like doing the laundry, going to the store, and so on. You get the picture.

Now, prioritize them by numbering them one through five, and you'll sleep more soundly knowing you have a clear plan. Keep your list visible—next to the coffee machine works for me. When you wake up, tackle the list starting with number one. Focus on completing each task before moving to the next. It's fine if some tasks take longer; just keep at it until they're done. Prioritizing the most important tasks ensures that you're making significant progress.

If you commit to this disciplined approach, you might not complete all five tasks every single day, but I guarantee you'll be far more effective nevertheless. You'll tackle what really needs to be done in the right order, and that's what counts. It's possible that the fifth item on your list might linger for a while, even ten days or more, but the crucial part is ensuring the top priorities are always accomplished. This process builds a disciplined routine that evolves into a powerful habit, propelling you toward your goals and personal growth.

This concept for enhancing our effectiveness with activities is remarkably straightforward. It helps us zero in on what truly needs to be accomplished. Many people I know sit down at their computers and simply drift through their day, reacting to whatever comes their way, without any clear direction or purpose. If they're employees, they're often just handling whatever tasks arise, rather than focusing on a specific outcome.

In today's world, it's easy to let emails and texts dictate and shape our day. But that shouldn't be our reality. Of course, we'll encounter urgent actions that need attention, but if we stay focused on our priorities by working through our list, we'll see some significant benefits. First, we'll boost our productivity and get more done. And if our work is tied to income, we'll likely see an increase in our earnings as well.

Here's the second benefit: I like to call it "freedom of headspace." When you have a clear plan for the day, you experience a sense of mental clarity. You're not bogged down by stress or anxiety about forgetting tasks because you've already addressed them the night before. This mental freedom lets you be more present and mindful, which enhances your overall well-being and helps create a balanced life.

Organizing Priorities

When it comes to prioritizing, the key question is this: What should take precedence? Is it the task that will bring in the most money, or the one that will bring you the most joy?

Here's how I see it: For entrepreneurs, the priority is clear—focus on what will generate income and pave the way for success. If you're in sales, your top priority should be centered on making sales. Ask yourself: How will I secure a sale today? Who should I reach out to? Will I spend the first hour of my day prospecting? The specifics will vary for each of us, but identifying the top few priorities is usually straightforward.

The remaining items on your list can be important but don't require immediate attention.

In the eighties and nineties, people relied on time management tools like Filofaxes, Day-Timers, and specialized planners. Today, there are countless digital apps for the same purpose. But here's the truth: We don't need to complicate the process. A simple priority list can be incredibly effective. As previously highlighted, the danger lies in getting stuck in endless planning without taking action. That's why I love this concept of five things so much.

My father had a saying for handling big tasks: "Reduce it to the ridiculous." He'd break down huge goals into smaller, more manageable parts. For example, if he had an annual income goal, he'd use his calculator to divide that number into monthly, weekly, daily, and even hourly targets. This approach made the big goal feel much more attainable and manageable. Keeping tasks simple often leads to the best results.

What you're reading in this book might seem too simple or even too easy. That's exactly how it's intended to be. Often, we overcomplicate our strategies, trying to make them seem more sophisticated than they need to be. That complexity can become a roadblock and prevent us from taking action. Simplifying tasks makes them more achievable. When something feels straight-forward, we think, "I can do that," and we dive right in. That's when productivity starts to take off.

This approach isn't just effective on a personal level, it's powerful for business as well. If you're leading a team, get everyone on board with this tool. Keep it simple and watch how much more your team accomplishes.

Let me share my own experience. By using this list of five, I typically knock out everything I need to do first thing in the morning. I focus intensely on each task until it's completed. This approach frees up more of my day for exercise, joyful activities, or whatever else I enjoy. Without that list, I could easily end up at the computer, lost in trivial tasks. But with a clear list of priorities that push me closer to my goals, I stay focused and get things done. When I follow this method, I not only feel better about myself but also see a significant boost in productivity.

At the end of the day, many people will say, "I really worked hard today." And they might have—no doubt about that. But the real question is, did they achieve much? Did they intentionally create joy in their day? There's a crucial difference between being effective and just staying busy. One person might put in long hours without tackling the most important tasks, while someone using this method could accomplish twice or even three times as much in less time. Effectiveness is about focusing on what truly matters, not just working hard for the sake of it.

There is a critical difference between effectiveness and mere doing.

I witnessed these results firsthand in the commission world. Back when I was heavily involved in affiliate promotions, I often found myself leading the pack by a significant margin. Despite earning a substantial income, I wasn't putting in long hours; in fact, I was working just a couple of hours a day. My success came from having a clear list of tasks, knowing exactly who I needed to reach out to, and following a well-defined strategy. Meanwhile, others were burning the candle at both ends, working from morning till night, and they still weren't making nearly as much money as I was. The key was in how effectively I managed my activities and focused my efforts.

We need to shift our focus to working smarter, not just harder. My father always championed the idea of enjoying life, and he knew that working hard wasn't the only answer. In fact, he loved to point out that working hard is actually the worst way to earn money. Sure, there are times when hard work is essential, but working smarter is equally crucial. That's how you can ultimately exit the rat race and get your money being put to work for you.

This straightforward list of five is a prime example of working smart. It helps you zero in on what truly matters. It's not about complexity; it's about clarity. What's crucial for your bottom line? What's vital for your success? What do you need daily to experience joy?

Prioritize, tackle the top item, and move forward. By adopting this approach, you'll see a remarkable boost in effectiveness in no time. Embrace this simple strategy, and you'll find that your results—and your life—transform for the better.

One person who truly embodied this approach was Gina Hayden, my father's assistant for nearly forty years.

Gina is one of the most effective individuals I've ever known. When she'd set her sights on a task, her focus was nothing short of laser sharp. She was a tremendous asset to my father. She played a crucial role in developing all his programs and ensuring everything stayed on course. They kept each other aligned, but Gina's effectiveness was truly remarkable. It was inspiring to see her balance my father's dynamic style with her own precision, creating a synergy that drove extraordinary results.

While I recommend preparing your list of five tasks the night before, it's best not to do it right before bed. Doing so can leave your mind restless and preoccupied. Instead, tackle this task at the end of your workday. I prefer to make my list before leaving my desk—sometimes even as early as noon. This way, I can think ahead about what needs to be accomplished the next day, jot it all down, and set it aside. This allows you to enjoy your evening without the worry of forgetting something.

When you go to bed, you'll have peace of mind knowing exactly what awaits you in the morning. Then, when you rise, you'll be ready to dive right in.

I'll say it again because it's so important and so many people miss this point: Sometimes, we over-complicate strategies, which can be a barrier to getting started. Simplicity is often the key. When tasks are easy, we're more likely to take action. I've found that focusing on my five things list allows me to accomplish my goals quickly and gives me more time for other activities. With a clear list, I stay focused, productive, and satisfied.

Key Points

- Time can't be managed; activities can be.
- Prepare a list of five goal-focused activities he night before.
- Start with the top priority on your list the next day and work your way down.
- This five-item list will help clear your mind and reduce mental clutter.

- By concentrating on your priorities, you'll create more free time in your day.
- We achieve greater effectiveness when we control our daily direction, rather than letting the day dictate our actions.

9

ATTITUDE

As I mentioned in the introduction, my father started to study the material of American radio speaker and author Earl Nightingale when I was a young boy. Earl had a wildly famous recording entitled "The Magic Word." This record sold over a million copies in the 1960s and revealed the word everyone needs to understand for achieving success—that word was *attitude*. I'm pretty sure I have heard that recording thousands of times.

I was taught the importance and power of attitude early on, straight from Earl Nightingale. The constant repetition of that one recording left a lasting impression and taught me early on the vital role that attitude plays in achieving success.

Earl Nightingale said the magic word was attitude because attitude is everything. It is the way we look at life. Our attitude shows the world the person we have decided to become. Our attitude is a combination of our thoughts, our feelings, and our actions. It plays a pivotal role in shaping and directing our lives.

The best part is that our attitude is our choice the moment we become aware that it's dynamic—it's not fixed. You're not going to feel good all the time—no one does. If you did, you wouldn't appreciate it because the low feelings help us recognize and enjoy the high ones. There will always be highs and lows, like the ebb and flow of tides and the rising and setting of the sun and moon. Understanding this concept makes it easier to navigate the lows with a good attitude—the tide will turn. And at any given moment in time, any day, no matter what's happening, with this awareness, we can choose our attitude.

We don't have to let our current circumstances or surroundings dictate our outlook. Our attitude can be as positive as we want, regardless of what's happening around us. That's up to us. When we choose to have a positive attitude and see the world in a positive light, the world responds positively. Conversely, if we choose to view the world negatively, the world will reflect that negativity back to us. "Your word is your wand" is another statement that comes to mind which is very true.

We all know people who are always positive and upbeat; they consistently look for the good in their circumstances and are pleasant to be around. They have enjoyable personalities. On the other hand, we also know people who constantly focus on the negative. They always see what's wrong and, as a result, attract more negativity into their lives. Even when something good happens, they find the negative aspect. As a result, they create more negativity in their lives.

Some of this habitual nature of one's personal attitude can be attributed to conditioning. As we all know, people grow up in vastly different environments. If you grew up with parents who are negative Nellys and Nasty Neds, it's likely that their attitudes conditioned your own.

However, we still have control over how we view life. With this in your awareness, you can choose to give less time and energy to negative thoughts and negative people. These things will always be around, but if you don't attach yourself to these negative ideas, you won't go down the path of a lower vibration. This includes recognizing but dismissing negative self-talk. You don't have to make negativity your identity. Instead, you can observe it with curiosity and set it aside as you focus on something more positive.

I have always looked at Oprah Winfrey as someone who has a wonderful attitude. She did not come from a very good environment, but she did not let that define who she was. Although she had some positive people in her life, she had many negative people in her life too. But she was able to get herself out of that environment, and she chose to look at the world in a positive way. She looked for possibility. She has done her best to positively influence the world in her interviews and other activities. She's dedicated her public life to spread better in the world. That's a gift that many have benefited from.

Oprah is a wonderful example of someone most people are familiar with. She has shown the world that anyone can do incredible things. You can make an incredible sum of money if that's what you wish. You can make a big difference if that's what you wish. Where we come from, our circumstances—none of that really matters if we have the focus, the will, and the persistence to look for the good and keep moving forward. Discipline and persistence will bend anything in our favor, and Oprah has been persistent all her life. She has proven that you can achieve beyond what you have imagined.

Inspirational speaker Jim Rohn said, "You are the average of the five people you spend the most time with." That means no matter what environment we come from, we can choose whom we spend time with. Along these lines, my father taught that, while we cannot choose our biological family, we can and should choose everyone else. So why not choose well?

Select people to be in your personal and professional life who are upbeat, always smiling, looking for the good side of things, and who intentionally choose a better way of living. Seek out people who know more than you know. You don't have to be the smartest person in the room. Sometimes it's better to be the opposite. If you're not the smartest one in the room, you could learn from those around you.

You are the average of the five people you spend the most time with.

Make sure that you surround yourself with upbeat, positive people, because you're going to pick up that attitude. There is a scientific phenomenon called group coherence. You will pick up whatever you surround yourself with, and likewise, others will pick up what you are putting out.

We have a choice. It is up to us to choose how we want to be, whom we want to be with, and how we want to act in this world. Yes, outside influences will always be there, positive and negative. But at the end of the day, it's our choice as to how we look at and deal with what is around us.

Attitude is the name of the game. As Earl Nightingale said, it's the magic word. It is the key component to getting on in this world for better or for worse.

It's true that young children can be in situations that they wouldn't choose. But once you become an adult, you have the power to choose, and you can start to choose the course of your life. Ideally, you'll recycle any bad experiences into powerful wisdom absent of long-lasting emotional traumas. That is why I brought up Oprah Winfrey, as she is a true testament to what is possible.

With friends, we certainly have a lot of choice, but some people have unsupportive or downright negative family members. In these cases they might say, "They're my family, and I love them. But at the same time, every time we get together, I feel diminished, and my mood sinks."

Sometimes the people who are the closest to us can be the cruelest. They know us, so they'll point out our flaws and cut us down. They'll say, "Who are you to think that you can reach those goals?"

Sometimes the people who are the closest to us can be the cruelest.

I've learned that in these situations, these family members are just showing you their own limitations. Their viewpoint is not necessarily correct; in fact, it almost certainly isn't. It's based on their own personal knowledge and experiences, and their individual attitudes, temperaments, and moods. We don't have to accept those views. If we do accept them, again, that's a choice. Many times, though false, their feedback can be coming from a genuine place of intention to protect you. Other times, it could be a result of jealousy or trauma. Regardless, it's important you recognize that you are the only one who knows what's right for you and what you're capable of.

When I'm about to be around people like that, before I get into the situation, I take a moment. I close my eyes, and I feel myself putting a kind of shield around my body and mind. I protect myself. I go in knowing that they may try to cut me down, and I remind myself that that's their stuff and not mine. It's up to me to accept it or not, and I choose not to accept it. I stay strong throughout those conversations. Often, I will get to a point where I simply feel sorry for them because they are trapped in a prison of their own making. They don't know what they don't know.

When you go into negative situations with that energy, I'm not going to say it won't affect you, but it won't affect you as deeply because you will go prepared, stronger, and armed. If I were to give you solid advice about this type of situation, it would be to avoid getting into an argument or a back-and-forth with negative people. I've often found that these interactions work best if you just nod your head and change the subject. What you resist, persists. People will not change their perspectives unless they're in a higher vibration and positive emotional state. So steer the conversation to something more positive and generally a different subject altogether.

With this method you're not engaging in their stuff, you're just letting it pass, realizing where it's coming from and knowing this is not a battle worth fighting. Again, you have a choice either to take on negativity or let it bounce off you like water off a duck's back.

Some situations are harder to extricate yourself from than others. If you are in an organization, you may have a difficult or tyrannical boss. If you report to somebody like that and it's causing you stress, it might be best to look for another position somewhere else so that you don't have to subject yourself to that type of abuse. The bottom line is it will affect you eventually. It is impossible to separate your emotional health from your physical health, so seek a positive change sooner rather than later. In my opinion, all dis-ease starts in the mind and emotions.

If you can't change jobs or make the required change immediately, it may be best to set up boundaries regarding what you are willing and not willing to do, and I wouldn't cross those boundaries. If you are doing your job and doing it properly, there's nothing for the difficult boss to attack you on. You should take responsibility for what you have to do, make sure it's done, and have boundaries set to protect yourself. But, at the end of the day, I would look for a better situation with a healthier work environment. You can find an organization that you'd love to work with—or start your own. When it comes to attitude, the only attitude you can control is your own.

Another issue can arise when we're changing, growing, and starting to do bigger things. We may feel judged, sometimes by the people closest to us—or people we've looked up to.

We discussed this previously. When we are changing, we're inadvertently and naturally forcing others to change their view of us. People generally don't like to be changed, especially when somebody else is forcing change upon them. So some people will accept it and be happy for you, while others won't like it and try to pull you backward. In the end, it comes back to the same idea: That's their stuff. You don't need to take it on. Recognize what's going on, treat them with compassion and understanding, and stay on course to be your best self and achieve your dreams.

When You're in Dire Circumstances

Negative situations don't always have to do with other people. You may be experiencing poor health, physically or mentally. Many people in our country are dealing with anxiety, depression, and other psychological issues. With physical problems, some are temporary while others might be more permanent. A person could, for example, be diagnosed with multiple sclerosis or something even more dire, like terminal cancer. How can you do your best to maintain a positive attitude in these circumstances?

Personally, I can think of some people who have had a great attitude through dire circumstances. They have a bright light within them. During the last days of his life, my father knew he was dying. He was in a lot of pain, but you would have never known it unless you were close to him. He still had a great attitude. He knew he was going, and he was ready to go, but what was most important to him was to make sure that everybody close to him knew how he felt about them. Even though he was suffering, he was doing whatever he could to encourage everybody around him.

I have private notes of things that he said to me that will last me for the rest of my lifetime. He had a wonderful attitude. Anybody who was in his presence during that time witnessed what it means to maintain a good attitude.

I have a close friend who is going through cancer treatment right now. The odds are getting better, but they were not great at the start. Through it all, he has had the most wonderful attitude. Going through chemotherapy and radiation, he has remained upbeat, he was smiling, and he did whatever he could for his family while he had the energy to do it. He doesn't complain; he just smiles and does whatever he can for his family.

It comes down to what I've been talking about over and over: We have a choice. Even when our health is not great, we have a choice in how to act. We can let it bring us down and bring others down around us, or we can choose to keep a positive attitude through it all. Of course, there are circumstances in this world that we can't control. Health and disease may be among them. But what we can control is our attitude and how we behave and treat others while we go through it. If we want to leave a gift to those closest to us while we're suffering though poor health, it could be the gift of a positive attitude.

A Model for Turnaround

I know a man who lives outside of Toronto. His name is Bruce, and he's the kindest man you'd ever want to meet. Some years ago, he was in business with his brother. His brother and his nephew were killed in a car crash. It took this fellow down. He went into a deep depression; he was in a terrible place. He was losing money and was about to lose his business. And he didn't care, because he'd given up caring about anything.

My father met this man during that dark time in his life and started to work with him. He really liked the guy. He helped Bruce to focus on the better things in his life. He taught him to look at the gift of the relationship and all the years he did get to enjoy with his brother and his nephew, and to focus on the positive aspects of where his business could go.

My father worked with him on his mindset and attitude for quite a while. Bruce took my father's message to heart and did the work to change his attitude and find his joy. Fortunately, he slowly began to rise from the darkness he had been living in.

The message here is that Bruce knew he was in trouble, so he searched for a mentor and followed the advice given. He learned to recognize how his thoughts and attitude were holding him down, and he did the work to create positive and life-saving change.

Bruce and I have remained friends, and his turn-around has been fascinating to watch. He is a role model for me. I've seen that man go through hard times. He continues to focus on the positive side of life. He also studies every day. Every time I talk to him, he tells me what he's reading, what he's studying, what he's doing, and he's always upbeat. It's a great way to show up in the world.

Do I think it is easy for Bruce? No I don't; life happens. I think it's a choice that he makes every day when he gets out of bed. It's become a way of being for him to choose to take on life with a productive attitude. Every day, we get to choose how we're going to approach life that day; and over time, choosing good becomes a habit, even when it's not the easy choice.

We can choose to let negative people or events control us and take us down. We can also choose to have a better outlook by thinking, How can I look at this from a better viewpoint? That's what Bruce has done. He's one of the best examples that I've seen of the power of transforming your attitude.

A positive attitude comes naturally to me, as I've had over sixty years of practice, raised to understand the difference between a good attitude and a bad attitude and conditioned by my father among others in the personal development industry. It's very rare that you'll find me feeling down, and even if I do, I don't stay there long. That's not to say I haven't faced challenges or bad moments, but, overall, I maintain a great attitude, often described as looking at life through rose-colored glasses.

While some may argue that this perspective is unrealistic or accuse me of being a Pollyanna, I choose to disagree. I believe we can look for the good in everything; it's a conscious decision. We don't have to agree with or like everything that happens, but we can opt not to focus on the negative. With awareness, we can intentionally view life positively, regardless of the circumstances. As my father would say, "Any dummy can tell me what's wrong; try thinking and tell me what's right."

**We can look at life through
rose-colored glasses.**

I know that not everybody was brought up the same way that I was. Nevertheless, from this moment on, you possess the necessary awareness to live like I do, and you can choose to look for the good. If you start to do that, you'll start to see things differently, and you will start to attract better into your life. As my father used to love to say, *better* is a very good word.

As I mentioned earlier, Wayne Dyer's quote is really fantastic. Study it and ask yourself what he really meant. Wayne said: "When you change the way you look at things, the things you look at change."

Extroverts and Introverts

Alongside the personal development movement launched by figures such as Napoleon Hill, Dale Carnegie, and Earl Nightingale, there has been a parallel growth in the understanding of human psychological and neurological complexity. Perhaps the most familiar discovery has been the polarity between extrovert and introvert in the individual character. Some people seem to be more naturally wired to be extroverted—outward-oriented—while others are more naturally wired to be introverted—inward-oriented.

Often a positive attitude is associated with the outgoing, friendly, gregarious person, which would appear to favor the extrovert. We must ask how introverts can cultivate this positive attitude.

To some extent, I think this is merely a matter of external appearances. Extroverts are stereotypically seen as positive. If you're an introvert, you may have a good attitude, but other people may not see you that way by sheer fact you may not be voicing that attitude outwardly as much.

To speak personally again, I'm more of an extrovert now, but for the longest time, I was an introvert, and I still have a lot of introverted ways about me. If you didn't know me especially in my earlier days, you might not know that I'm looking at the world in a positive way, but I am and always have.

In short, I don't think it matters if you're labeled an extrovert or introvert because that is all it is—a label. Our attitude is on display in how we treat ourselves and others. Our attitude shapes how we see our life and the world. It shows in the way we carry ourselves and how we engage with others. Being an introvert or extrovert is neither good nor bad; it just is. If we were all the same, it would be a pretty boring world.

Morning and Night People

Here's another way the issue of attitude can be sliced: the morning person versus the night person. I'm a morning person myself, but I don't think it's necessarily easier to be positive if you're a morning person. There are early birds, and there are night owls. We're all wired differently. Many people hold the philosophy that early risers are more successful, and while that's true for me, I know plenty of night owls who also rock their businesses and achievements.

The key comes back to attitude. We may have times when we need to operate opposite of our natural early— or late—rhythms. This can throw many people out of whack, but the reality is we don't have to be grumpy when it's not our time of day. We can still choose our thoughts and actions. If you're a night owl and you've got to get up at 5:00 a.m., you might be a little sluggish. You might not want to be active. You can still choose to do something with vigor and with a smile on your face. It's a choice. Recognize your natural rhythm is more like a habit and a preference, and not a static part of your personality or identity.

We don't have to let personality types, or even body types, dictate how we act. We're all in different surroundings. We all have different things going on in our life, good and bad. In any case, if we let our circumstances or environment dictate our attitude, we're not in the driver's seat. We're letting the world control us. If we let the world control us, life won't be very much fun. We're just going to be rolling with whatever's happening and not make progress toward anything more meaningful than what we are living in this moment.

**If we let the world control us,
life won't be very much fun.**

If we stay in control, if we're in the driver's seat, and if we are focused on being the best version of who we are at all times, no matter what time of day it is or what our energy level is, I think we're going to have a great attitude. If we're focused on being the best version of us, we're always going to be looking for the good, and we're always going to be doing our best. Is my best at ten at night going to be the same as a night owl's best at ten at night? Absolutely not. But my best can still be my best, and it's living from this intention that makes all the difference.

Since I am a morning person, one thing I do—and if you are a morning person, I highly recommend this—is get up every morning, look at the horizon, and wait for the sunrise. I wait for the sun to pop up over the hills. The second it peeks out, I look at it, and I say good morning. Seeing the sun come up in the morning reinforces my sense that it's a new day, it's a fresh day, it's a new start. It's a habit I've gotten into. Both my wife and I like to do this. We sit with our cup of coffee, and we look out on the horizon, waiting for the sun to rise.

This is a wonderful practice for the mind and for our bodies. It also has a positive effect on the brain. Many studies show that getting sunlight in your eyes first thing in the day will help you sleep better at night and keep your energy from dropping off during the day.

Other habits to maintain my positive attitude include the practices I've already discussed, such as using affirmations and life scripts. It's also valuable to read, listen to, or study positive material, which includes listening to a beautiful piece of music that moves you.

I saw how my father studied all his life. I'll be the first to admit that I don't study the more extreme way he studied, but I do study. I read some excellent books, and I certainly love to watch inspirational talks on You-Tube.

Feeding your brain with positive material will automatically help you shift your perspective to looking at life in a more positive and healthy way. It will help you keep on track in the direction of your dreams and desires. And you often will stumble on gold nuggets that you didn't know you didn't know, and that you didn't realize would forever change your life.

The key message here is this: Do not let your current circumstances or surroundings dictate the way you look at life. You always have a choice.

I suggest you choose to look at life through rose-colored glasses, like I do. Habitually pick a great attitude instead of a terrible attitude. Remember, it's up to you. Make sure especially not to let other people control your attitude. Why? Because you're the one in control. Remember, you're the star of your own movie. No matter what is happening, always stay in control. Some people and situations can be rather aggressive, so I won't say it's always easy, but it will get easier if you maintain a positive attitude with intent.

Would you like to know what another fun thing is about understanding this? It's that you are not only going to understand yourself better as you progress down this path, you are also going to understand others better. You will be able to tell immediately the kinds of thoughts and ideas that people are involved with through their words and actions. When you understand yourself better, you also understand the rest of the world better—because, really deep down, we're all human and we're all fundamentally the same.

**No one is in charge of your happiness
and positive attitude except you.**

Key Points

- *Attitude* is the magic word.
- No matter what environment we're in, we can choose whom we spend time with.
- Avoid negative people.
- By changing, we're forcing others to modify their view of us, which can trigger resistance. This is their stuff and not ours.
- Our attitude starts with a decision to move through life looking for and finding the good.

10

MMFI

This lesson, the MMFI concept, has been a cornerstone of my life since I was nine. It's a paradigm I've consistently applied both personally and professionally, and it's proven to be remarkably effective.

Interestingly, I was unknowingly applying the MMFI concept in my business life without fully realizing what I was doing. It wasn't until I was twenty-seven, during my first year in real estate, that I applied this simple concept with conscious intention.

I remember being at a seminar in Palm Springs led by Mike Ferry, a prominent real estate trainer, with around two thousand agents packed into a ballroom. I was sitting right at the front, and it seemed Mike had heard about my success in sales. To my surprise, he called me up on stage. At first, I was a bit taken aback, unsure of what was happening.

Mike said, "You're young and relatively new to the business, yet you're outpacing many seasoned professionals. Share with us how you're achieving such impressive results."

His question almost instantly took me back to when I was nine years old. We had just moved to Chicago, and my father was about to begin working with Earl Nightingale and the Nightingale Conant Corporation. You see, I was born in Toronto and started school there, but soon after, we relocated to London, where I started a new school. A year later, we moved back to a different area of Toronto, and I started yet another school. Then, before I knew it, we were in Chicago, and I found myself in my fourth school by fourth grade. I dreaded the idea of being the new kid once again because I was finding starting over to be difficult.

I can clearly remember sitting with Dad in the den of our new Chicago home sharing my apprehension about being the new kid at school. My father's advice was straightforward but deeply impactful. He told me, "Brian, here's what you need to do. Imagine these four letters written across the forehead of everyone you're talking to: MMFI."

I asked him, "What does that mean?"

He replied, "It means, Make Me Feel Important. If you can make everyone you interact with feel valued, seen, and heard, you'll make friends and build connections quickly. It's a positive way to navigate the world with ease."

He continued, "It's actually quite simple. When you're talking with someone, show genuine interest in them. Ask questions, be engaged, and really listen. Don't focus on what you'll say next; just be present in the conversation. Sometimes, all it takes is a sincere compliment. Even if you don't particularly like someone, you can always find something positive to say. Whatever it is, make sure you're making the other person feel important, seen, and heard."

MMFI: Make Me Feel Important

I started doing that, and I made friends easily and got along wonderfully. I did the same thing when I got my first job, and when I started in business. When I had clients in real estate, I was interested in them, listened to them, and made them feel as if they were the only clients I had.

You know, there are times when someone shares a significant accomplishment, and the response is, "Oh, I did that, too, and I did it even better." Have you ever encountered that? One-upping only serves to overshadow the other person's achievement; it diminishes the value of their story. I've always steered clear of that trap, even if I've had a similar success. Instead, I focus on celebrating their story and genuinely engaging with what they've shared. It's made a world of difference in my life.

At a party or gathering, we've all run into that one person who just goes on and on about themselves.

They're so wrapped up in their own story that they don't even bother to ask about you. It can be draining, right? Or have you been with the person who is always looking around the room? Speaking to you but you can feel they are really not engaged.

Then, you meet someone else who turns the tables. They're genuinely interested in you, asking questions, making eye contact, and really engaging in the conversation. Suddenly, the interaction is meaningful, and you experience a real connection. They make you feel valued and seen. It's a refreshing contrast and a powerful reminder of how much of a difference it makes when we focus on making others feel important.

This step is straightforward. It ties back to a key concept I've discussed before: being present. When you're with someone, immerse yourself fully in that moment. Let go of everything else that's happening around you and focus solely on the interaction at hand. By doing this, you ensure that everyone you meet leaves feeling uplifted and valued. It's about making a positive impact and leaving others with the impression that their time with you was a true enhancement to their day.

Be present in the moment with whomever you're with.

Make it a priority to make everyone you encounter feel important. It could be the barista at your coffee shop or the cashier at the grocery store. Sometimes, it's as simple as offering a warm smile that makes them feel acknowledged. Ask them, "How's your day going?"—and don't just ask nonchalantly; genuinely care. Look them in the eye and show real interest. Let them feel you in earnest. Notice and appreciate the good they're doing, whether through a heartfelt compliment or a word of thanks.

There are countless ways to make someone feel valued and seen, and it starts with your sincere effort to connect. If you notice someone having a bad day, ask yourself how you could do something seemingly small that could brighten their world, even if just for a few seconds as they interact with you.

Make it a priority to ensure everyone you interact with feels important—truly seen and heard. When you do this, you'll find great success in business, and clients will be drawn to you and your positive energy. People naturally gravitate toward genuine, uplifting connections.

So, back to the story about when Mike Ferry called me up on stage and asked about my success. The lesson that came to mind was MMFI, and that's exactly what I shared: "I make every client feel like they're the most important person in the world."

Because of this approach, I didn't just gain loyal clients who were eager to buy or sell, but they also began referring all their friends and family to me. My business grew effortlessly because I treated each client as if they truly mattered. I made sure they felt my genuine care through my presence and attentiveness.

The MMFI concept became a cornerstone of my life, and it has served me incredibly well. I see this same quality in my children, especially in my son Danny. He has a remarkable way of leaving everyone with a sense of increase. He makes each person he meets feel important and valued, as if they're his closest friend from the very start. And he does this with complete authenticity.

This principle harks back to one of the great classics of personal development: Dale Carnegie's *How to Win Friends & Influence People*. At its core, that book's timeless message is all about making others feel significant.

Loving Loved Ones

While I've been discussing this principle in the context of meeting new people, it's even more vital when it comes to our loved ones and family. We often take those we care about for granted, failing to make them feel as valued and important as they deserve. It's all too easy to let those closest to us become part of the landscape, and sometimes we end up treating strangers better than we treat our own spouse or partner.

If you've been in a long-term relationship, you might find yourself falling into this trap. We need to consciously make an effort to show our special people how much they matter. Imagine what your life would be like without them and let that awareness fuel your gratitude and appreciation. Make it a point to ensure they know how much they mean to you every single day.

The Skill of Active Listening

Active listening is a fundamental part of this principle. It's not just about hearing words; it's about truly engaging with what someone is saying. When we listen attentively, we don't have to stress over our next response because we genuinely understand where the other person is coming from. The right response will naturally follow; there's nothing to worry about preparing for.

On the other hand, if we're only hearing words while preoccupied with what we're going to say next, the conversation lacks depth and connection. Now, please make a note of what I'm about to say. Perhaps highlight this line with your favorite highlighter: Hearing is done with the ears, but listening is done with the heart.

Active listening means being fully present and emotionally engaged in the exchange, which allows us to respond thoughtfully and meaningfully. This kind of deep listening creates a richer, more fulfilling interaction for both parties.

Let's revisit a core idea from earlier in this book: While words hold significance, feelings hold even greater power. When you're truly engaged with someone and listening with genuine intent, they can sense it. They might not be able to pinpoint exactly what's happening consciously, but they feel it deeply at the subconscious level. This emotional connection transforms conversations, making them far more profound and meaningful. It's this authentic engagement that deepens connections and enriches every interaction. This is how relationships flourish.

Words are important, but feelings are more important.

Stop fixating on what you're going to say next—it's not the most important thing. The real key is whether you're genuinely hearing and listening to the other person. When I'm in a conversation, I follow a simple rule: I ask myself, Is what I'm about to say necessary, kind, or helpful? Is it coming from my heart? This keeps the focus on meaningful communication.

Years ago, Dad was invited to lead a sales meeting for a group of radio stations in Canada. Unfortunately, he couldn't attend, so he suggested, "Well, perhaps my son could step in." At the time, I had just started out in real estate but had already shown great success in sales. I was in my twenties, and speaking to a group was completely new territory for me. Despite my discomfort, I agreed to take on the challenge.

Without much experience or conviction in my message, the presentation didn't go well. I had a solid message, but my delivery fell short. I spoke from my head, not my heart, because I was more concerned with how I was being perceived than with actually connecting with my audience. My focus was on myself rather than on them.

As I began speaking, I shared an important lesson: When you're on a sales call, it's crucial to approach the conversation with genuine love and warmth for the person you're talking to. Speak to them about your product or service, but let that conversation be infused with an authentic, energetic kindness. They might not articulate it, but they'll sense that positive energy and feel a warmth from you. Even if you misspeak, they'll still be drawn to you because they'll resonate with the good feelings you project.

I remember the puzzled looks from the audience; they probably expected conventional sales tips, but I was offering something different—a way of being. If I were in that same position today, I'd convey the same message, but with far more conviction and from a place of heartfelt understanding, rather than just intellectual knowledge. Ironically, I'd practice the exact same advice I was preaching, which I failed to do as a rookie speaker back then.

Feel love from your heart for a person as you're speaking to them.

That's something I've really mastered over time. I no longer focus heavily on the exact words I use; instead, I concentrate on the feeling I convey. When your goal is to project a genuine warmth and positive energy toward whoever you're speaking with, that energy will be felt. It's that feeling that truly makes a difference.

Imagine you're coming from a place of agitation and need. Your self-talk is filled with desperation: "I need to make a sale because my mortgage is overdue, and my car might be repossessed." This creates a negative vibration that's palpable. Even if you're saying all the right things and offering exactly what your prospective client needs, your underlying desperation is felt at the heart-to-heart, subconscious level.

As your prospect, they sense something isn't right, and it turns them off, so they don't make the purchase. However, if you'd have used the same words while coming from a place of genuine love and positive energy, the prospect would have felt that warmth, responding positively and being far more likely to want to buy from you. It's simply natural.

Certainly, someone can use MMFI as a mere technique without the genuine feeling of love backing it, putting on a facade of care to get what they want. But people are adept at sensing insincerity; they can spot phoniness from a mile away. When practicing MMFI, it's crucial to be genuinely energetically connected with the other person. You're not just going through the motions—you're truly making them feel important. If you're merely treating it as an exercise, they'll pick up on it, and it will undermine your entire intention. Even if they make a purchase, there very likely will be buyer's remorse setting in soon.

The key is authenticity. The more genuine and truly interested we are in the other person, the better our interactions will be. It's that unseen connection, the silent communication, that carries the most weight. Remember: Words are important, but feeling is more important. Put your intention on operating heart to heart. This applies to digital conversations just as much as in-person interactions.

Talking Good about Someone

Dad and I were both early risers, so we'd start our days by talking in the morning. We developed a habit I like to call, "Talking good about someone behind their back." We'd choose a person and focus on their positive qualities, sharing all the great things about them. Of course, that person never knew we were discussing them. This practice uplifted our energy and made us feel great, simply because we were focused on the good in others.

Think about the difference this can have in your life with interactions. While most people engage in common gossip and negative thoughts, you can be "that guy" or "that gal" who changes the directions of a conversation and speak good about people behind their back.

Often, I'd follow up with an email or message to that person, saying, "Dad and I were talking about you today, and it was all good." It had a way of brightening their day.

In an earlier chapter, I mentioned the couple who run the air-conditioning business. A few years back, I received a text from the wife saying, "I just wanted to let you know that we're talking good about you behind your back."

They had heard the message I shared from the stage about the practice my father and I did and had embraced it themselves. That gesture meant more to me than almost anything else. It's often about acknowledging someone's actions long after they've occurred—making them evergreen and a long-lasting, positively charged emotional memory. What a powerful way to touch someone's heart and make a real difference in their day.

My father was a true master of MMFI. Watching him at seminars was always a highlight. In a room of a thousand people, he'd step down from the stage, place his hand on the shoulder of an attendee, and strike up a conversation with them, even if he didn't know who they were. He had this incredible ability to make that person feel truly special, and, at the same time, he brought everyone else into the moment. That's a remarkable gift.

My father always made time for people. I'd often be the one picking him up from his hotel room to take him to an event, and there would be folks wanting to snap a picture with him. He never rushed past anyone; he'd pause, chat for a moment, and take that picture.

That's real magic. When we positively and genuinely touch lives, we're not just doing a good job—we're living from a place of higher awareness and understanding of life itself.

My father adopted this concept from Wallace D. Wattles, who called it "leaving an impression of increase." It is simply this: What can you do to leave everyone who comes in contact with you feeling better because they were in your presence?

Key Points

- MMFI: Make Me Feel Important.
- Honor others' stories: Avoid overshadowing their experiences.
- Be present: Fully engage with whomever you're with.
- Listen deeply: Effective communication hinges on true active listening.
- Connect energetically: Ensure you're genuinely connected to the other person.
- Operate heart to heart, in person, digitally and otherwise.

11

WHAT YOU FOCUS ON

The subject of this chapter has been touched on in many classic works on self-development. In 1903, James Allen published *As a Man Thinketh*. The title comes from Proverbs 23:7: "As he thinketh in his heart, so is he."

Earl Nightingale also covered this concept in *The Strangest Secret*. This secret is ages-old, but has recently achieved New Age status and popularity. The concept is simple: What we focus our energy, thoughts, and emotions on is what we bring into our lives.

Even though this awareness is gaining more and more headlines these days, many people still do just the opposite—they direct their energy toward what's wrong or missing, and, consequently, they attract more negativity. We often desire something, but our focus is on its negative aspects—or on its absence. We want good health, yet we dwell on illness. We seek wealth, but our thoughts are consumed with debt and lack.

Listen to how people speak, and you'll hear it clearly. They use language that undermines their potential: "I can't do that," "That's not me," "I'm not good at this." In saying these things, they are thinking and feeling thoughts in harmony with the statements and therefore attracting their (lack of) results.

We attract into our lives whatever we focus on and emotionally invest our energy in. It might sound too simple, but that's the reality. We're like magnets, drawing to us whatever we concentrate on.

Even when things aren't unfolding as you'd like, it's vitally important to monitor your thoughts and consciously redirect them, concentrating on your desires, the actions you can take to achieve them, and what you can do today to advance. The more energy you channel into the positive aspects of life and your goals, the more you'll attract positive experiences in harmony with this energy.

What we focus on, we will bring into our life.

I'm not going to promise that applying this principle will transform your life overnight. In fact, just as it takes time for a freight train to stop, change direction, and gain momentum in the new direction, so operates life when you start to set new goals and intentions. So when you dedicate your energy to being aware of your thoughts, you will begin to notice a shift, and this freight train of desire will start to pick up steam.

You can expect that your mood might lighten, you may find yourself laughing more, and you'll start to see the goodness in those around you. Over time, you'll realize that where you invest your energy is where you see results. It's therefore important to maintain positive momentum as best you can and minimize any seesawing back and forth between the positive and negative ways of being.

A year from now is coming, whether you're ready or not and whether you're positively focused or not. By focusing on what you want and directing positive energy toward it, you can create a drastically different reality in this coming year compared to what would happen by maintaining old, default patterns. On the other hand, if you dwell on what's not working or keep digging up the seeds you've started sowing in attempt to check on their progress, you'll likely find yourself stuck in the same place—or worse.

When we channel our energy toward what we desire, we're actively participating in its creation on a physical and metaphysical level. Metaphysical means "beyond physical" and today is explained by quantum physics.

To put it simply: Everything is energy—our bodies, our thoughts, our emotions, and the patterns dispersed throughout. We attract into our lives whatever we invest our time and energy in.

The book and film by Rhonda Byrne titled *The Secret* explored the law of attraction and the immense power of our thoughts. She based this work heavily on Wallace D. Wattles's book, *The Science of Getting Rich*. However, *The Secret* failed to highlight a crucial component, which is action. To truly create change in our bodies and in the physical world we are a part of, action is essential. Based on my personal experiences as well as witnessing the positive and negative manifestations of millions of people, action is an integral part of the process and a key aspect of creating the results we want for our lives that can't be left out.

Many people have very specific outcomes they wish for, but they don't take the necessary steps to make them a reality. To truly bring something into your life, you must let go of any negative stories you've been telling yourself, and you must realize that while you work in concert with the Universe and other people to bring good about, you are in the driver's seat and you must put your foot on the gas pedal. Focus deliberately on your true desire and invest your energy into it through intentional, concrete actions. Through these actions, you translate your energy into the physical world, and you receive exactly what you want.

Action is the key to manifesting your desires.

Our thinking shapes our attitude, which I touched on in chapter 9. This attitude is essentially how we view the world. This brings us back to a core theme of this book: the power of choice. We have the power to choose whether to focus on the positive or the negative. Whatever we direct our focus toward is what we invite into our lives. I may have mentioned choice a million times throughout this book—and that's definitely been on purpose!

Seeing Red Mazdas Everywhere

One fascinating feature of the mind, often linked to the reticular activating system (RAS) in the brain, is its tendency to find what it's focused on. For instance, if you're considering buying a red Mazda (or any other color and type of vehicle), you'll begin to notice red Mazdas everywhere you look. It's not that these cars were not there before and have suddenly appeared; they were always there, but you were unaware of them because they didn't hold your interest. Once red Mazdas become a focal point for your mind, you'll start seeing them all around you. Try it out and see how many you notice the next time you're out where vehicles are driving about.

The mind tends to find what it's looking for.

This example illustrates the focus principle perfectly. When you consciously decide to buy a Mazda and want your new car to be red, you start noticing them everywhere. But this principle operates even with subconscious thoughts. If we dwell on something we don't want, even if we're not verbalizing it—but we're feeling it—our mind brings it into our awareness and often makes the thought a reality.

On the flip side, when we focus on what we truly desire, especially when we start to habitually trigger positive feelings about this desire, we begin to see the opportunities that have always been there but went unnoticed. By concentrating on these opportunities and taking action, we start achieving what we're focused on.

Just as social media algorithms serve up more of what catches your interest—because you lingered on an ad, searched for a specific keyword phrase, or clicked a link—the Universe operates on a similar principle. It reflects back to you what you're focusing on. It's the all-original, organic type of algorithm, existing since the beginning of time.

What shows up in your life is a direct manifestation of where your attention is directed, what you're feeling, and what you're thinking about. The Universe's "algorithm" mirrors your focus, bringing more of those thoughts and feelings into your reality.

The mind possesses immense power. Dad used to say, "There is only one mind—just one. It's an illusion that you and I are separate from one another. We're individual expressions of the same mind."

If you go into a room, pick somebody who is turned away from you and start focusing on them. As you concentrate on them, envision them turning around and gazing in your direction. You'll notice them begin to fidget and move, and soon enough, they'll turn around to meet your gaze. They sense the intensity of your attention, even though you may be nowhere near them physically.

Ever been thinking about someone and then get a call or text from them on your phone? Same principle, just a greater distance between you. We are all connected. Everything is energy.

While everyone is inherently drawing into their lives whatever their minds fixate on, the challenge lies in maintaining focus on what you truly desire rather than on what you wish to avoid. The majority of people are fixated on what they don't want. They concentrate on what's wrong or lacking, and this focus becomes their reality. Moreover, they often align with others who share this negative outlook, creating a collective mindset of lower consciousness—of a lower nature of vibration. As the group grows, so does the negativity, with individuals reinforcing each other's limiting beliefs and thoughts.

In comparison, fewer people focus on what they do want and give energy to the positive. Although I say fewer, I still think there's a lot who are in the healthy habit of focusing on what they want.

Many people out there are doing all kinds of positive activities in the world. They are focused on the good. They're focused on what they want and what they're doing. They don't let their outside circumstances or other people dictate how they view and think about the world. There are perfect examples all over the place of people who are in control of their thoughts and actions. Take notice and learn from them. Model them.

When you encounter someone deeply committed to their goals, focusing on their desires and taking deliberate actions to achieve them, it's noticeable. These folks naturally stand out, and you might find yourself drawn to their energy. They don't let external circumstances or outside opinions sway their perspective. Take notice of these exceptional examples; these are people who have mastered their thoughts and actions, demonstrating control and intention in their lives.

This kind of focused, directed action is a powerful strength—what I like to call a superpower. Everyone possesses it to some extent. Even those who seem trapped in negative circumstances are demonstrating this ability, albeit in the wrong direction—they are fixated on what they don't want.

Just as you can grow and develop a muscle, disciplined focus and intentional action can be developed too. It requires commitment, time, faith, and persistence. The key is understanding that this mindset demands effort. It's far easier to see, hear, and speak about the negative aspects of life because it requires no thought. To steer your life in a positive direction, you must think and consciously choose which thoughts to focus on.

I'm not sure why life works this way, I just know it does. We can embrace this awareness and use it to our advantage—and the world's advantage too.

Calm Inner Knowing

An important point here is recognizing what we can control. If we fixate on events outside our control, we'll be tossed around like a pinball in a machine. Here's a fundamental truth: You can only control yourself. While you can influence and persuade others positively through your own actions, you cannot control them. Your role is to be the example.

Concentrate on what you can control, direct your efforts there, and give it your all. Stay focused on your own path. By doing so, you'll begin to take command of your life and shape your reality effectively.

I'm applying this principle to a new program I'm launching. It's a significant endeavor, and I won't deny it's a bit intimidating to put myself out there. But because of my experience, I have a deep, unwavering confidence that it's going to turn out exceptionally well. My intention is to serve and assist others through this work, and because of that, I'm certain of my success. I'm betting on myself.

I could choose to dwell on the fear of potential failure, or I can embrace the certainty that it's going to succeed and be well received. My focus is on the positive outcome, and that mindset feels far more empowering than worrying about failure. I'm focused on what I can control, which drives my actions in the right direction.

This brings us to another key aspect of this practice: maintaining that inner knowing with a sense of calm. When you possess a confident, calm inner knowing, you're less affected by the chaos around you.

When you catch yourself in a cycle of negative thinking, it's important to recognize when it's counterproductive and not solving anything. Give yourself permission to break away from that line of thinking. Use the exercises shared throughout this book to pull yourself back out of it and get back on track. And remember to always be gentle with yourself.

Redirect your attention from excessive thinking to engaging your senses. This might involve practices like meditation, gardening, or simply stepping outside to immerse yourself in nature—feel the wind, the sun, or the rain, listen to the ambient sounds, and connect with the ground beneath you. The objective is to interrupt your thought patterns and restore a sense of calm and clarity. Do something that brings you joy.

I believe that a calm inner knowing acts as an open invitation for the good you desire to enter your life. It's like welcoming positive energy and opportunities. In contrast, when you operate from a place of frenzy, chaos, and stress, you push goodness away. Forceful, anxious energy only serves to block the natural flow of positive experiences. Force always negates progress.

There does seem to be a part of the mind that's naturally attracted to the dramatic and sensational. You can observe this phenomenon on the highway, where even a minor fender bender on the shoulder draws everyone's attention. As drivers slow down to rubberneck, they create what's known as a "gaper's block," causing a significant traffic jam.

This same tendency is evident on social media, in news headlines, and in various other areas of life. It's almost instinctive: We're often drawn more to the sensational and shocking rather than to the inspiring, positive, and enriching. Why? Once again, I'm not sure. But I sure am glad to be aware of it.

To counteract this tendency, we must consciously seek the positive side of life. It's quite simple once you commit to it. For instance, try going to YouTube and searching for content on topics like attitude or uplifting stories. By focusing on positive themes, you'll start discovering valuable and inspiring content. In doing so, you can shift your algorithm toward more uplifting and enriching material, rather than dwelling on the sensational and negative. Both digitally and organically, you'll begin to align your algorithms to success.

The inspirational speaker Simon Sinek is a great example of these qualities. He loudly embodies intentional and unwavering optimism and holds a deep belief in our collective ability to shape a bright future. Watching his videos is truly inspiring; his positivity is something I personally connect with. Of course, not everyone will resonate with him, and that's perfectly fine. You might find someone else who aligns more closely with your own values and aspirations. The exciting part is discovering those individuals who reflect the person you are choosing to become.

It's a great idea to seek these people out and start to model them. Don't endeavor to be them. Rather, notice the positive traits you like and implement those into your own unique personality and existence.

We must take charge of the material we consume daily. If we don't, algorithms and people around us will dictate our exposure, continually presenting us with negativity. Be proactive in seeking positive content and strive to maintain that uplifting vibration. Know that, yes, it's about feeling better—but it's also about attracting better.

Here's the fascinating truth: Our brains function much like these algorithms. They continuously deliver what we focus on by reinforcing our search and maintaining our chosen perspective. Unless we intentionally disrupt this pattern by shifting our focus, we'll keep receiving more of the same. Remember the freight train analogy. Start turning your freight train in the direction of your desires and know, in time with consistency, you'll be cruising right along.

My Father's Turning Point

As you know by now, my father was my biggest role model by far. Observing him throughout my life, I learned the importance of choosing how you present yourself to the world. Since the day I was born in 1961, I've been immersed in personal development. My father, a pioneering figure and a leading mind in this field, is regarded as one of the greatest thinkers of our time.

When Dad began in the industry, the business was vastly different from what we know today. He had to literally physically knock on doors and find any way possible to reach an audience. Today, with the internet, communication is much easier. This shift has likely contributed to the remarkable growth and expansion of the self-development and coaching world we now see.

In the early days, the challenges were numerous. I witnessed my father endure rejection, financial hardships, and various other obstacles, as the field of personal growth and development was not widely understood or embraced. Yet, he remained steadfast and persistent. He kept pushing forward, holding a clear vision of his goals. Deep down, he believed with all his heart that his message would make a difference and help people around the world.

A major turning point in my father's career was the release of *The Secret*. When that movie was released, it elevated him to a new level of visibility. Suddenly, he was on a much larger stage, reaching a far broader audience. This exposure was a game changer that propelled his message to a global audience and marked a significant milestone in his journey.

He couldn't have predicted what that turning point in his career would be, but he always held a clear vision and knew that it would come if he stayed focused, maintained his vision, and kept putting in the work. By the time *The Secret* was released, he was seventy-two years old, having already dedicated over forty years to his craft. On the way to his interview with Larry King in January 2017, his assistant Gina asked if he were nervous. Dad casually laughed and said, "No, I'm not nervous. I've been expecting this!"

To me, that's a remarkable illustration of faith and persistence and a steadfast vision, backed by a worthy ideal. Quitting was never an option for him. Instead, he remained committed. He was always looking for new ways to reach people and make a difference. He sure did find them, and they found him.

Whatever path you choose, pursue it with passion and remarkable dedication. Cultivate a deep, inner certainty that you will achieve your goal. Trust the processes and principles I've shared with you in this book to help get you there, supported by your daily action.

Do whatever it takes and refuse to let external circumstances or limited opinions cloud your vision—continue pressing forward. Your journey, marked by growth, joy, and a deeper understanding of your life and why you are here, will be the measure of your success along the way.

Know in your heart of hearts that you will get there.

It might unfold overnight, or it might take you until you're seventy-two. But if you're pursuing a grand vision that ignites your passion, the journey itself will be your success. Along the way, you will be learning and evolving, knowing that you're moving in the right direction. Your growth will come from both the challenges you face and the wins along the way. Embrace every bit of it with open arms and an open heart.

I find myself in a similar place now, engaging in pursuits I never imagined I'd take on. Driven by a grand vision and a significant goal, I'm stepping out of my comfort zone again and into the stretch zone of growth and learning.

I am paying close attention to how I start my day, knowing it sets the stage for everything that follows. I devote time to my gratitude journal, concentrating on what I'm thankful for—everything that is, everything that isn't, and the positive things on their way. I immerse myself in the abundance and beauty that surround me, truly feeling and appreciating it. I follow every single piece of advice personally that I've given you here inside this book.

I deliberately choose to operate from a place of generosity and goodwill, offering kindness simply because it feels right—not to receive something in return or out of obligation.

Each day, I write out my goal in detail, clearly defining what I'm striving for. I shift my focus away from doubt and refuse to let past results cloud my vision. I reaffirm my desired outcome, setting a clear and positive direction for the day. Then I take a moment to sit quietly, centering my thoughts on my objective and the reasons behind it, maintaining a calm and confident mindset.

I remind myself, "I have a deep, peaceful knowing that I will achieve this." I share this certainty with my wife Cory, too, often saying, "I have this calm inner knowing that things are going to turn out exceptionally well for us."

Statements like that ground us and instill a sense of expectation in the present moment. Even if you don't fully believe it at first, repeating your affirmations will gradually make you feel and believe it. By voicing these affirmations, you project an expectation into the world into your own subconscious and draw that idea into your current reality.

These practices broaden my perspective and make it easier for me to recognize opportunities and take intelligent action in the right direction. They attract what I need and fill me with a deep sense of purpose. I know they will do the same for you.

What are you focusing on each day? Are you concentrating on what you want, or are you dwelling on what you don't want? This is an important question to ask yourself. And ask it often!

Remember: You become what you think about.

Once again, ultimately, it comes down to choice. It's up to us to decide where we direct our focus. Ensure that you're focusing on what you truly want. Approach this with a sense of peace and calm, allowing it to deeply resonate with your heart. Embracing this heightened sense of self-awareness allows you to naturally and effortlessly attract what you desire. It's not the result of any single action but rather the outcome of the entire approach you've adopted.

One final component on this subject is our inner dialogue. How do you talk to yourself? Would you be friends with someone who talks to you the way you talk to yourself? Make sure you talk to yourself in a kind way, as any good friend would. That inner dialogue is a barometer for how we are thinking and what we will attract into our life.

Key Points

- The strangest secret: What we focus our energy on is what we attract into our lives.
- Active participation: By directing our energy toward our desires, we actively participate in their creation.
- Focused mind: The mind naturally seeks out what it focuses on.
- Inner certainty: A calm inner certainty enhances confidence and amplifies the effectiveness of our focus.
- Positive content: Seek positive content to shift your mental focus toward material that fosters growth.
- Consistent thoughts: You become what you consistently think about.

If you embrace these principles to harness the power of your thoughts, feelings, and actions, you will pave the way for a fulfilling and successful life—and you will open up access to a calm and joyful way of being right now.

12

ACT AS IF

Freedom comes when we stop being what other people think we should be and start acting like the person we really deep down want to be. *Act as if* is another principle that I learned from my father at a very young age, and it has been a valuable tool throughout my life.

Every one of us does new things. As humans we are always forging new ways, and none of us is an expert at anything immediately. It takes time to learn. My father always advised me, "When you go into any venture in life, you need to act as if you are the best at that venture. Be that person, and act as if you are that person. Soon, you will then become that person."

I've heard the expression, "Fake it till you make it," which shares a similar concept, but it carries a less favorable connotation. Faking it often lacks authenticity. In contrast, when you act as if you are truly embracing the role you aspire to, authenticity is palpable and noticeable. The key difference lies in the intention. Acting as if means you are intentionally stepping into the person you are taking steps to become, which is fundamentally different from simply faking it until you achieve success.

When you act as if, you're not merely putting on a facade for show; you're actively endeavoring to be who you desire to be for the positive impact it will have on everyone involved.

When I ventured into real estate sales in my twenties, I took my father's advice to heart. He said to approach sales as if I were the top agent in all of Toronto, right from the start. I was to treat my clients as if I were the best and deliver exceptional service. That's precisely what I did. As I said before, my initial clients had no clue I was new to the field. They believed I was an outstanding agent because I acted like one.

By embodying that role, I became that person. It might seem like a fairy tale, but our actions shape who we become. Acting as if shifts our mindset to align with higher-level thoughts and vibrations, and although it may initially feel like a role, soon it becomes who you truly are. This approach involves repetitive practice in your mind, which builds the confidence you need.

By adopting the mindset of being the best, you will, in time, become the best.

Impostor Syndrome

People today talk a lot about impostor syndrome. Essentially, impostor syndrome is when you feel self-doubt about your abilities and accomplishments, despite evidence to the contrary.

You may feel disconnected from the role you're occupying in life, as though you don't truly belong in that position. This experience can affect anyone no matter your social status, expertise, or level of success. However, if you look at anyone in a position of authority, at one point in time, they weren't that person. They had to act as if they were, and then they became that person through their actions. Their self-image had to evolve to align with this new identity they were stepping into, and they gave themselves the space and permission to do so.

Impostor syndrome is a feeling of not being there yet. The best way to overcome it is to act as if you are already there. By being that person, you're not an impostor, you're on the road to mastery. This approach isn't about ignoring what you don't know; rather, it's about using your self-awareness to step into an improved version of yourself and building on what you do know. Again, you're not doing it for show. You're doing it to create genuine outcomes for everyone involved.

Essentially, feeling like an impostor stems from a self-image problem. Many individuals are more than capable and overqualified, yet they hesitate to reach their full potential due to their self-image. They experience significant anxiety when stretching beyond their comfort zone or even while fulfilling their current roles. This low self-image often results from the limiting definitions placed on them by family, culture, religion, and personal experiences. When you start to question your beliefs and ideas about yourself, you can begin to make breakthroughs. Remember that our beliefs about ourselves stem from thoughts that we keep thinking, so when we change our thoughts, we change who we are.

Here's the important message to remember: If your goal is truly significant, it will pull you to move through discomfort and anxiety. It will drive you to step out of your comfort zone and do what's necessary. It will feel like something you can't resist, even though you may feel some fear.

This is a fundamental aspect of acting as if. When you embrace the role of the person you aspire to be because it aligns with your goal and stretches you beyond your usual limits, you naturally evolve into that person. It won't always be easy, but the transition will become more manageable as you remain committed. The intense feelings of fear won't last as long and eventually will diminish.

My father and his suits are an example of this. For as long as I can remember, Dad had a love for fine tailored suits.

Back in the early 1960s, when he first started an office cleaning business, he scraped together his last few

dollars to buy a wool suit. This was the one and only
suit he had for his first few years in business. It was
not of high quality, so you can imagine how scratchy
it would start to feel on his skin, especially during the
warmer summer months. He loved the look of it but got
tired of how it felt and, more importantly, he got tired
of the same look every day.

One day he heard an interview on the radio with
someone famous. It came out that this person had over
twenty custom-tailored suits in his closet. That really
shook my father. He said to himself, How wonderful
would that be? Until that time, he had never heard of
anyone with more than one, maybe two suits.

Something in that interview changed Dad's perspective.

He decided then and there that if he reached a specific sales target each month, he would go out and get
himself a custom-tailored suit. He honored that agree-
ment he made with himself, and it wasn't long before he
had a closet full of suits.

In the beginning, he had to act like the person
who deserved and could afford all those suits. But in
no time, he became that person. You would be hard-
pressed to find him dressed in anything else. Wearing
these well-made suits not only changed how he felt
about himself but also changed the way he carried himself. I remember him telling me that wearing those new
suits made him walk with purpose. He knew that the
people around him started to see him differently, too,
and he liked that.

**If you want something, if that goal is
big enough, the pursuit of that goal will
cause you to step through anxiety.**

To overcome feeling like an impostor, we must focus on enhancing our self-image. We need to affirm our own worthiness and take the necessary steps to genuinely feel it. If that means delving deeper into your studies, then do so. If you're aware of what's required but still feel anxious, craft a straightforward affirmation that supports this new image. Take whatever actions are needed to align your mind and spirit and fully embrace your role.

Indeed, stepping out of your comfort zone is essential to build upon your existing successes and *act as if* is a deliberate step out of your comfort zone. It is you crafting your life with intentional direction rather than leaving it to chance. It is taking purposeful steps toward your goal, and every step in the right direction, no matter how small, contributes to your progress. What won't work is doing nothing or repeating the same old patterns—that is how you stay stuck exactly where you are or, worse, go backward.

Obstacles and failures are part of the journey. When they occur, it's important to learn from them without dwelling on them. Examine what happened and why, then continue moving forward. Look for the lessons and choose to lean into the good. My father had a practice he learned from businessman and author W. Clement

Stone: Regardless of whether the outcome was good or bad, he would say, "That's good," and then he'd keep moving forward. There's always something good to find when you're looking for it.

When I released my first book, *My Father Knew the Secret,* I set the goal of becoming a best-selling author and acted as if I had already achieved that status. I pursued every opportunity, appeared on podcasts, and participated in interviews. I was determined to do whatever it took to spread the word. Through that relentless effort and belief, I reached my goal of becoming a best-selling author. No matter the obstacles, I kept pushing forward. When things didn't go as planned, I let it go and continued focusing on my goal.

In the publishing world, many people release a book and expect it to automatically succeed. They fall short of taking the necessary actions. They might sell only a few hundred copies and then become disheartened.

For me, settling for less was never an option. Based on what I learned from my father, I understood that by acting as if I were already that person, I would naturally take the actions a best-selling author would take, and I did. And by doing so, I became that person.

The challenge often lies in falling into the trap of getting fixated on the "how." We think we need to master every detail and have a complete, comprehensive plan before we can become that person. We either let existing obstacles stop us or create new ones ourselves.

The essential truth is this: When we act as if we are already that person, the obstacles will still be there. They might impede us at times, but they won't stop us permanently. We'll discover ways to navigate around them, and each step we take will reveal the next. It's crucial to trust the process and keep moving forward.

Obstacles may block us temporarily, but they won't block us forever.

Acting as if is a simple concept, but don't underestimate its power. You need to harness your belief in yourself. Know with absolute certainty that you can achieve your goal. Each of us is striving to enhance our lives and circumstances, and you're reading this book because you're committed to that improvement. Acting as if you're already the person you aspire to be is one of the most effective and expedient ways to elevate your life.

What will happen when you start acting as if? Well, for one, you will encounter critics. People will observe and question, saying things like, "You're not really that person. Why are you pretending?" When I started acting as if I was the best salesperson in real estate as a newbie, I faced many critics with questions like that.

The key is this: If you persist in acting as if you are that person, eventually you will become that person, and others will recognize you as such. This is where persistence, fortitude, and strength come into play. When you face resistance and negativity, especially from those who doubt you, stay committed to your vision. If your goal is truly significant and you desire it deeply, you won't let others deter you from achieving it.

Everyone who has achieved greatness has first acted as if they were already that person before they truly became them. Take actors, for example. When they step into a role, they fully embody that character. In the same way, you need to step into your desired role as if you are already that person. Over time, this act will become so ingrained that it will take over your life. You'll evolve into that person, and when you look back, you may be surprised at how seamlessly and swiftly the transformation occurred.

Of course, it's necessary to draw some distinctions here. Acting as if doesn't mean pretending to be something you're not or claiming qualifications you don't possess. For example, you can't pass yourself off as a doctor without the proper medical training. That's not acting as if; that's deceit. Authentic acting as if involves stepping into your desired role while remaining grounded in your genuine skills and knowledge.

When we talk about acting as if, it's essential that you have a solid foundation in what you're doing; it's about advancing from where you are now and becoming a greater version of yourself. You should be stepping into the role of an expert in an area where you have already been investing time and effort. Authenticity means you're not deceiving anyone; you're genuinely engaged in the field, even if you're not yet the absolute top expert. By acting as if you are the best, you align yourself with the professional ethics and standards that define the top performers in that field.

Stepping Through the Fear

Acting as if demands courage, which often goes unsaid. Courage isn't about being free from fear; it's about acknowledging the presence of fear and moving through it anyway. It means pressing on despite self-doubt and apprehension.

In recent years, I've taken on numerous challenges that frightened me, but I understood that facing these fears was necessary to evolve into the person I aspired to be. When acting like that improved version of myself, I had to face and step through fear. I encourage you to do the same. The more you do it, the easier it becomes to pull through.

Begin by asking yourself how badly you want to improve. If your desire is strong enough, you will be driven to do whatever is necessary to achieve it.

I've faced many days where I had to summon my courage and push through discomfort. I found that, despite the intense fear I felt in those moments, once I took the necessary actions, it was rarely as daunting as my mind had anticipated. While some outcomes weren't perfect, I achieved victory simply by moving forward. Each time I stepped through fear, the fear diminished, and the next challenge seemed less intimidating. With each success, I built confidence.

Although it wasn't always easy, the role gradually became more manageable and eventually effortless. The fear dissipated as I continued to take action.

To overcome doubt, we need to transform our thinking, especially our self-talk. Shift away from negativity and connect with your inner cheerleader. Dig deep and demand more from yourself. Get those nervous butterflies into formation and use them as fuel to propel you forward, fueling your pursuit of your deepest desires.

This ties back to chapter 2 on setting goals. Ensure your goal is sufficiently ambitious to inspire you to persist, even when it feels impossible and fear sets in.

Remember, this is all about your thinking and feeling, and how you perceive those thoughts and feelings. What defines something as good or bad? Your thinking. That's it. What turns something into a feeling of excitement or fear? Your perception. That's it. When you alter the way you look at things, you shift your perspective, and the situation transforms.

Keep Moving Forward

An important part of this process is something I learned from my father: Never think you know it all. Keep studying. Keep working. Keep moving forward. Keep chasing that dream. Keep doing what is required. It goes back to that analogy of building a house one brick at a time. You are making progress and getting stronger with each step. You are betting on yourself. When you can bet on yourself consistently, you will win.

A significant fear I had to face was speaking on stage. With a father like Bob Proctor, I imagined everyone was wondering, "Is he as good as Bob?" Even though public speaking was essential to achieving my goals, it was a terrifying challenge for me.

When I first began, I had a conversation with my dad about this fear. He shared an important insight that transformed my approach. He said, "Brian, if you're afraid of getting on stage, it's because you're focused on what others might think of you. But if you shift your focus to teaching them something valuable, speaking from your heart, and channeling your energy into serving them, the fear will dissolve. You'll find you have nothing to fear."

It was absolutely accurate. When I took a step back and reflected, I realized that my fear stemmed from the thought, Oh, God, what will they think of me? So now, I don't compare myself to my father because I'm not Bob Proctor. I'm Brian Proctor, with my own unique approach and style of teaching.

My father was truly one of a kind, with a distinct way of speaking and teaching. If I were to mimic him, I wouldn't be true to myself. Authenticity is key. Without it, I can't be impactful or make a meaningful difference.

I focused on becoming the best version of myself, which I continue to do every day. I became committed to teaching in my own way and sharing my story authentically. My focus has always been on empowering others to improve their lives. This focus has allowed me to act despite my fears. I remind myself that the fear, doubt, and worry I experience are just thoughts—and that I don't need to believe every thought I think. By acknowledging these feelings and moving beyond them, I affirm my faith in my goal and my confidence in my ability to make a difference for others.

No matter what we're doing, there's always room for improvement. When I step onstage or join a podcast, I commit to being the best I can be in that moment. I focus on being present and giving my all. Good things come my way because I'm willing to bet on myself and navigate through uncertainty. Is this a way of being you'd like to implement into your life?

Be the best you can be, right here, right now.

Stick with It

A great example of *acting as if* I want to share is about Milt Campbell, a dear friend of my father's. Although he's no longer with us, he was an extraordinary man. Milt was an Olympic athlete who won the gold medal in the decathlon in 1956. I'll always remember what Milt told me.

He said, "When I was in high school, I wasn't the top athlete, but I persevered." That persistence led him to win the gold medal in the decathlon at the Olympics. There were other kids who were more talented, but they didn't have Milt's drive or commitment. They didn't want it as badly as he did.

That taught me a powerful lesson in persistence. Milt Campbell reached the pinnacle of his field not because he was the most talented, but because he remained committed. He put in the necessary work and didn't give up. His relentless dedication made him the best.

The essence of this chapter is about embracing what's true for you. It's about being authentic and aligning with your higher self. This isn't about being a fraud—far from it—but rather stepping into the person you aspire to become. When you act as if you are already that person, you are simply aligning with your chosen path. By embodying this future self, you will naturally take the actions that person would take. Through these actions, you will transform into that person and ultimately become who you envision yourself to be.

The ability to hold the vision and act as if, despite how it feels when the sharpness of others' opinions cuts deeply, is when you know you are aligning your behavior with your belief.

Anyone who has reached the top of their field has done so because they put in the effort, and a significant part of that effort involved acting as if they were already the best. They worked diligently, learned from their experiences, and made adjustments as necessary. I encourage you to take the same approach. Determine what you want to achieve. Start by acting as if you are already that person, and, in time, you will become that person.

Key Points

- Approach every endeavor by acting as if you are already the best.
- If your goal truly matters to you, you will push yourself and demand more from yourself. Soon enough, the goal will pull you.
- Venture beyond your comfort zone.
- Focus on your successes and use them as a foundation to build upon.
- Courage isn't about the absence of fear; it's about the willingness to move forward despite it.

FINAL THOUGHTS

As we come to the end of this journey together, I hope you've gained valuable insights and practical tools to transform your life. The principles and practices I've discussed are not just theories; they are proven strategies that can lead to a more fulfilling, successful, and joyful existence.

Embrace the Journey

Remember, personal growth is a continuous journey, not a destination. It's also a choice. Every step you take, no matter how small, brings you closer to your goals. Embrace each moment and celebrate your progress. Success is built one step at a time, much like the bricklayer who patiently constructs a house brick by brick.

Focus on the Present

Living in the present moment is one of the most powerful ways to enhance your life. It allows you to fully experience and appreciate your journey. When you focus on the now, you reduce anxiety about the future and regrets about the past. Each day offers a new opportunity to take action and make positive changes. And joy becomes a priority and a consistent way of being.

Small Steps Lead to Big Achievements

Consistently taking small, deliberate steps toward your goals creates momentum and leads to significant accomplishments over time. Whether it's writing a few hundred words daily, making a single sales call, or practicing gratitude, these small actions compound into substantial progress. One small step toward your goal every day adds up to 365 small steps in a year—and that will lead you to something big.

Get Physical

Get into a regular habit of doing something physical. Your body and mind will be sharper because of it. You will have more energy to do the activities that bring you joy.

Positive Attitude and Gratitude

Maintaining a positive attitude and practicing gratitude are foundational to a successful and happy life. They shift your perspective and allow you to see opportunities rather than obstacles. Gratitude attracts more good into your life and helps you stay grounded and content. Always stay focused on what you want with intention and speak to yourself with a kind and encouraging voice.

Setting and Achieving Goals
Set clear, inspiring goals that challenge you and push you out of your comfort zone. Write them down, visualize them, and take daily actions toward achieving them. Remember, the journey to achieving your goal is as important as the goal itself. The journey is where growth and transformation happen.

An Impression of Increase
Make sure you leave everyone you come into contact with feeling better because they were in your presence.

Overcome Challenges
Challenges and setbacks are inevitable, but they are also opportunities for growth. Stay resilient, learn from your experiences, and keep moving forward. Your ability to overcome obstacles and adapt to change will define your success.

Live Authentically
Strive to live an authentic life, true to yourself and your values. Authenticity fosters deeper connections with others and brings greater satisfaction and peace. When you live authentically, you inspire those around you to do the same. Remember that acting as if is still living

authentically when done with the right intentions and strategy.

Support and Encourage Others

As you work on improving your own life, look for ways to support and uplift those around you. Encourage others to pursue their goals and dreams. Your positive influence can create a ripple effect, bringing better into the world.

*   *   *

You've taken some sizable steps toward creating a better life by engaging with this book. Keep the momentum going. Implement the principles and practices you've learned, and don't be afraid to revisit them as needed. Your journey is unique, and your growth will continue as long as you remain committed and open to learning.

Believe in yourself and your potential. You have the power to create the life you desire. Stay focused, stay positive, and keep taking those small steps every day. Success with happiness is not only possible, it's within your reach.

Thank you for allowing me to be a part of your journey. Here's to your continued growth, success, and joy.

Now, go out and live your best life!

ABOUT THE AUTHOR

Brian Proctor brings a truly unique perspective to the field of personal development as the son of the legendary Bob Proctor, a pioneer in the self-development industry. From an early age, Brian was immersed in the principles of success and positive thinking, surrounded by many of the founding figures of personal development, both past and present. These relationships provided him with a rare, firsthand understanding of the key ingredients to success.

For nearly thirty years, Brian had the extraordinary privilege of working alongside his father, accompanying him on some of the world's largest stages. This experience deeply ingrained in him the power and value of a positive mindset—a lesson he carries with him to this day. Watching his father teach and inspire millions around the globe, Brian developed a profound appreciation for the impact that mindset and self-belief can have on one's life.

While working with his father, Brian discovered his niche in marketing and business development. In the early years of the internet, he recognized the potential of digital platforms and devised a groundbreaking idea to build an email list by creating value. This strategy ultimately evolved into a massive worldwide platform for his father to share his teachings. Brian's foresight in email list building set Bob Proctor's company up for unparalleled success, positioning them as early adopters of what would soon become an industry standard.

Contributing to his father's legacy, Brian is a best-selling author in his own right with *My Father Knew the Secret.* The secret refers to the law of attraction—principles that Bob Proctor espoused long before Rhonda Byrne's *The Secret* book and movie, which is what attracted her to include Bob's voice in her works.

Together with his wife, Cory Kelly Proctor, Brian runs a successful coaching business called Proctor's Principles. They teach people from all corners of the globe how to live better, more fulfilling lives. Through this program, they help individuals step out of their comfort zones and embrace the life they've always dreamed of.

Brian and Cory have made their home at the south end of Puget Sound in Washington State, where they are living their dream of a life spent near the water, surrounded by nature's beauty. Their passion for helping others achieve their goals is matched only by their love for the tranquil, inspiring environment they now call home.

For more about Brian Proctor and his work, visit www.brianproctor.com.